W9-BJI-419

LESSON SIXTEEN

MORE ABOUT "SOME" AND "ANY"

We know already that "some" or "any" is in French *du, de l', de la* or *des*.

du fromage; de l'eau; de l'argent; de la bière; des hommes

But sometimes "some" or "any" is translated in French by *de* whatever the gender of the noun and no matter whether it is singular or plural.

COMPARE these two: "some French wine" and "some good wine". Now *français*, being an adjective of nationality, comes after the noun in French, but *bon*, being a short and common adjective, comes before the noun. This gives us our rule. If the adjective comes AFTER the noun (nationality, colour, long or uncommon adjectives) "some" ("any") is *du, de l', de la* or *des*. If the adjective comes BEFORE the noun then "some" ("any") is *de* (or *d'*).

Examples:

du vin français; but *de bon vin*
des arbres verts, (some) green trees; but *de grands arbres*, (some) tall trees
de l'argent anglais, (some) English money
de belles pommes; but *des pommes rouges*

Provided that one adjective comes before the noun *de* is used, whether another adjective comes after the same noun or not.

de vieux chapeaux—de vieux chapeaux gris; but *des chapeaux gris*

You can have two adjectives both before the noun.

de pauvres petits animaux

If two adjectives both have to come after the noun it is best to put *et* between them.

une foule pittoresque et bruyante, a picturesque and noisy crowd

There is one other instance when this same thing happens.

63

If the verb is negative (that is used with "not"), then again "some" ("any") is *de* (or *d'*).

We have some money. *Nous avons de l'argent.*
We haven't any (we have no) money. *Nous n'avons pas d'argent.*
Il y a du lait dans la bouteille. There is some milk in the bottle.
Il n'y a pas de lait dans la bouteille. There isn't any milk in the bottle.

How to say "I used to be" and "I used to have".

In the last lesson we saw that the Imperfect Tenses of all verbs have the same endings: *-ais, -ais, -ait, -ions, -iez* and *-aient*.

HERE, then, is the Imperfect of "to have" and also of "to be".

j'avais, I used to have (I had)	*j'étais,* I used to be (I was).
tu avais	*tu étais*
il avait	*il était*
nous avions	*nous étions*
vous aviez	*vous étiez*
ils avaient	*ils étaient*

We saw in Lesson Seven that *j'ai trouvé* can mean either "I have found" or "I found". In Lesson Fifteen we saw that if "I found" really means "I was finding" or "I used to find" we use the Imperfect, *je trouvais*. In the same way, *j'ai été* can mean "I have been" or "I was". But if "I was" really means "I used to be", then we should use *j'étais*.

SIMILARLY "I had" in the sense of "I used to have" or "I was having" is *j'avais*, but "I (have) had" is *j'ai eu* (*eu* is the Past Participle of *avoir*).

J'avais un chien. I had (used to have) a dog.
Hier j'ai eu mal à la tête. Yesterday I had a headache.

Word List 16

monsieur, sir, Mr.	*M. Blanc,* Mr. White
un monsieur, a man, a gentleman	*Mme Blanc,* Mrs. White
des messieurs, some gentlemen	*Mlle Blanc,* Miss White
Madame, madam, Mrs.	*une chambre à un (deux) lit(s),* a
mesdames, ladies	single (double) room
mademoiselle, miss, young lady	*libre,* free, vacant
mesdemoiselles, young ladies	*le petit déjeuner,* breakfast
occupé, occupied, taken	*aimer,* to like, to love
payer, to pay, to pay for	

Exercise 16 (*a*)

Put into English:

1. Il y avait de grands arbres et de belles fleurs dans le jardin de la maison où nous demeurions. 2. Si vous n'avez pas d'argent je vous prêterai cinq francs pour acheter du vin rouge. 3. En regardant par ma fenêtre j'ai vu un officier et une douzaine de soldats français qui marchaient vers la gare. 4. Je suis sûr qu'ils allaient monter dans le train qui arrive ici à trois heures. 5. En montant dans l'autobus, j'ai vu notre voisine qui achetait au marché des pommes vertes. 6. Je n'aime pas les pommes vertes. Un jour j'ai mangé un kilogramme de pommes vertes et j'ai passé deux jours au lit. 7. Quand nous étions petits nous allions souvent au bord de la mer. 8. Nous passions nos vacances chez un fermier; il n'avait pas de moutons, mais il avait de très belles vaches. 9. Je suis sûr que cet homme a bu trop de vin: il tombera dans le fleuve. 10. Avez-vous une chambre à un lit qui donne sur la mer? Non, madame, mais nous avons une belle chambre à deux lits qui donne sur le jardin. 11. Cette

place, madame, est occupée, mais il y a ici une chaise qui est libre. 12. Je vous ai dit déjà, M. Dupont, que je n'ai pas d'argent à vous prêter.

Exercise 16 (b)

Put into French:

1. Mr. Green and his wife used to live in our house. Another gentleman, Mr. Black, was their neighbour. 2. We never had any dogs when we were young. 3. We lived in a town and there were many cars in our street. 4. My uncle had some beautiful horses. I used to look at them for (during) hours. 5. The double rooms are occupied, madame, but we have two nice (pretty) single rooms which are free. 6. The two gentlemen who spent the night here have taken the train for Paris this morning. 7. If you do not want to buy these newspapers, miss, I will lend them to Miss Dupont. 8. That good Mr. Dubois has brought you two dozen eggs and some white wine. 9. He told us that he had no money, but this morning he was buying (some) vegetables at the market. 10. If you walk as far as the church, you will meet Mr. and Mrs. Leclerc. 11. There are a crowd of children who are getting into a little boat. 12. Haven't you enough French money (in order) to pay (for) your breakfast?

Have a Try 16

Le directeur de la maison de commerce (*business firm*) où est employé M. Lebrun—le père de Jean—est malade. Pour cette raison M. Lebrun a décidé d'aller à Rouen à (*in*) sa place pour parler d'une affaire importante avec un client qui demeure dans l'ancienne capitale de la Normandie. M. Lebrun a eu la bonne idée d'inviter sa femme et les deux garçons, Jean et Charles, à aller avec lui. Naturellement Charles est très heureux d'accepter cette invitation qui lui donnera l'occasion (*the opportunity*) de visiter Rouen qui est une très belle ville et un centre industriel.

"Il y a un guide parmi les livres qui sont sur la table près de mon lit," dit (*says*) Mme Lebrun. "Je suis sûre que nous trouverons dans ce livre une liste des hôtels à Rouen, et je téléphonerai au bureau d'un des hôtels qui sont recommandés dans mon guide."

LESSON SEVENTEEN

HOW TO SAY "I SHOULD GIVE"

In Lesson Twelve we saw that to get the French for "I shall give" (Future) all we had to do was to add to the Infinitive *donner* the endings *-ai, -as, -a, -ons, -ez, -ont*.

Now in order to be able to say "I should give" all we need to do is to add to the Infinitive *donner* the endings *-ais, -ais, -ait, -ions, -iez, -aient*. Do you recognise these endings? They are exactly the same as those we used in forming the Imperfect. The only difference is that we got the Imperfect by knocking off the *-ant* of the participle *donnant* and adding the endings to the stem *donn-*. BUT to get the Conditional ("I should give") we add them to the Infinitive (just as we added *-ai*, etc., to the Infinitive to form the Future). Here for comparison are all three tenses:

Imperfect	Future	Conditional
je donnais, I was giving.	*je donnerai*, I shall give	*je donnerais* (I should give)
(*tu donnais*)	(*tu donneras*)	(*tu donnerais*)
il donnait	*il donnera*	*il donnerait*
nous donnions	*noud donnerons*	*nous donnerions*
vous donniez	*vous donnerez*	*vous donneriez*
ils donnaient	*ils donneront*	*ils donneraient*

The Conditional is so called because it is often used to show what would happen or what someone would do under certain conditions.

Si j'avais de l'argent, je vous donnerais un cadeau. If I had some money (but I haven't!) I would give you a present.

We have met the word *si* with the meaning of "so".

si grand, so big

It also means "if".

Meaning "so", *si* is never shortened when followed by a vowel. Meaning "if", it is shortened to *s'* when followed by an "i" but not otherwise.

si énorme, so enormous   *s'il est malade,* if he is ill

BUT

si elle est malade, if she is ill

Word List 17

la dame, the lady	*inviter (à)*, to invite (to)
le dîner, dinner	*attraper*, to catch
le poisson, fish	*tirer*, to pull, drag
le fruit, fruit	*penser*, to think
dîner, to dine, have dinner	

Exercise 17 (*a*)

Put into English:

1. Si vous êtes si malade, pourquoi avez-vous marché jusqu'au vieux château? 2. Nous allons visiter Mme Dubois. Si elle est chez elle, je l'inviterai à dîner avec nous à l'hôtel. 3. Pour le déjeuner hier nous avons eu du poisson et des fruits. 4. Ce petit garçon a attrapé un poisson si

énorme que j'ai pensé qu'il tomberait dans l'eau pendant qu'il le tirait à la surface. 5. Mme Leroux m'a dit qu'elle me prêterait dix francs pour acheter les billets. 6. Quand le temps était beau nous n'allions jamais au cinéma. 7. S'il ne désirait pas aller au bord de la mer, pourquoi ne l'a-t-il[1]

[1] *l'a*: *l'* = *it*, but in English "so" would be better.

pas dit? 8. Si toutes les places sont occupées, nous monter-
ons dans une autre voiture. 9. Ce monsieur-là est un ami
de mon cousin. Nous l'avons rencontré chez Mme Dupont.
10. Je n'étais pas sûr si vous arriveriez aujourd'hui ou
demain. 11. J'ai dit au fils du médecin qu'il ne gagnerait pas
sa vie, s'il ne travaillait pas à l'école. 12. Il y a une dame à la
porte qui désire parler avec Mme Lepic.

Exercise 17 (*b*)

Put into French:

1. You will find some fine fish (*plural*) at the market this
morning. 2. The shopkeeper told me that he has no vegetables, but he will bring us some big apples. 3. If I had
enough money, I would invite you to dine at the "White
Horse". 4. That old lady used to be a great actress. 5. No,
madam, there aren't any single rooms which look (give) on
to the sea. 6. I was sure that the policemen would not catch
the men who have stolen your car. 7. If she doesn't want to
go to the cinema, give me her ticket. 8. If she is so rich, why
does she not give fifteen francs to her son? 9. That fish will
pull him into the water if he catches it. 10. This place is
already occupied, sir. If you look (seek), you will find
another chair which is free. 11. How much red wine has he

drunk? Three bottles. 12. We were not sure when we
should arrive at the hotel. 13. He would not eat so much, if I
was not paying (for) his dinner.

Have a Try 17

En descendant du taxi. M. Lebrun regarde avec anxiété
l'horloge de la Gare. "Bon. Nous avons dix minutes avant
le départ du train." Il fait (*makes*) un signe à un porteur et
les quatre voyageurs lui donnent leurs bagages. Charles
remarque avec intérêt que le porteur les attache à une
courroie (*strap*) qu'il porte sur les épaules (*shoulders*).

"Nous allons à Rouen," dit (*says*) M. Lebrun, "par le
train de onze heures."

"Oui, monsieur. Si vous entrez dans le passage souterrain,
je vous chercherai à la barrière."

Au guichet (*booking-office*) M. Lebrun demande quatre
billets d'aller et retour de seconde classe. Ils trouvent leur
porteur à la barrière.

"A cette heure, monsieur, vous trouverez sans difficulté
des places."

En deux minutes ils sont assis dans un compartiment où il
n'y a pas d'autres voyageurs. Charles est très content parce
qu'il a une place de coin (*corner*). Mme Lebrun n'est pas si
contente. Elle regarde son mari d'un air de reproche
(*reproach*). "Vous avez donné trop d'argent au porteur.
Sommes-nous des touristes américains?"

LESSON EIGHTEEN

ABOUT NUMBERS

We already know (Lesson Eleven) the numbers up to twenty. Here is a further list:

vingt et un, 21	*trente et un*, 31
vingt-deux, 22	*trente-deux*, 32
vingt-trois, 23	*trente-neuf*, 39
vingt-quatre, 24	*quarante*, 40
vingt-cinq, 25	*quarante et un*, 41
vingt-six, 26	*quarante-deux*, 42
vingt-sept, 27	*cinquante*, 50
vingt-huit, 28	*cinquante et un*, 51
vingt-neuf, 29	*soixante*, 60
trente, 30	*soixante et un*, 61

NOTICE that in 21, 31, 41, 51 and 61 we have *et* between the *vingt* (etc.) and the *un*. In all the others there is no *et* but a - linking the two parts together. The *un* in these numbers becomes *une* with a feminine noun, but the other numbers do not alter.

41 bottles, *quarante et une bouteilles*
45 houses, *quarante-cinq maisons*
many houses, *beaucoup de maisons* (*de* after an adverb of quantity)
a dozen men, *une douzaine d'hommes* (*d'* after a noun of quantity)

How to Say "Which house?" or "What book?"

As we know already, "this book" in French is *ce livre* and "that house" is *cette maison*. But how are we to say, for instance, "What book?" or "Which house?" We know that in "the book which I have bought" "which" is *que*: *le livre que j'ai acheté*. But we want to be able to use "which" or "what" before a noun, just as we can translate "this" or "that", "these" and "those" before a noun by using *ce, cet, cette* or *ces*.

HERE are the words we need: "which" or "what" before a masculine noun is *quel* (sing.) or *quels* (plural). "Which" or "what" before a feminine noun is *quelle* (sing.) or *quelles* (plural).

Here are a few examples to show some of the ways in which "what" and "which" can be put into French:

> *Quel train avez-vous pris?* What train did you take (catch)?
> *Le train qui arrive ici à deux heures.* The train which gets here at two o'clock.
> *A quelle heure allez-vous à l'école?* (At) what time do you go to school?
> *Les fleurs que vous regardez sont des roses.* The flowers (which) you are looking at are (some) roses.
> *De quelles fleurs parlez-vous?* Of which flowers are you talking?

Word List 18

le couteau, knife	*couper*, to cut
la salle à manger, dining-room	*la distance*, distance
un auteur, author	*le prix*, price (*also* prize)
préférer, to prefer	*la classe*, class, class-room

Exercise 18 (*a*)

Put into English:

1. Avec quel couteau avez-vous coupé le pain? Avec ce couteau-là. 2. Où est mon journal? Quel journal? Le journal que je vous ai prêté hier. 3. Il y a déjà cinquante voyageurs assis dans la salle à manger de cet hôtel. Allons dîner chez nous. 4. Cet auteur a écrit quarante-sept livres. 5. La maison où nous demeurions était à une distance de vingt-neuf kilomètres de Tours. 6. Si vous allez à Tours vous trouverez douze ou treize grands châteaux à une petite distance de cette ville. 7. J'ai envoyé une carte-postale à mon ami. Il m'a écrit une lettre de trente-deux pages! 8. A quelle heure arriverons-nous à Paris? A trois heures. 9. A quel prix avez-vous acheté ce tableau? Je l'ai payé quarante-deux francs. 10. Quels fruits préférez-vous? J'aime beaucoup les pommes. 11. Combien de garçons y a-t-il dans votre classe? Il y a trente-sept garçons. 12. Avez-vous une bonne place dans votre classe? Oui, très bonne. Je suis assis près de la fenêtre!

Exercise 18 (*b*)

Put into French:

1. In the dining-room of the old castle the table is so big that there are places for forty or fifty men. 2. Which books have you taken? I took the two which were on the table. 3. Let us look for your friend. In which carriage is he? 4. Which books do you prefer? I don't like (the) books which are very long. 5. The farmer told me (said to me) that he has bought fifty-seven cows. 6. At what distance from Paris is your house? At thirty-five kilometres. 7. At which hotel shall we dine? At the "Black Horse". 8. The author of those books which you like used to be one of my friends. 9. I did not see your aunt at the café. At which table was she sitting? 10. At which hotel did you spend the night? At the Grand Hotel, which has a dozen double rooms. 11. At what price did you buy the tickets? At eleven francs. You will find that we have good seats (places). 12. What fish did you eat? I do not like fish; we prefer meat.

Have a Try 18

Pour Charles le voyage de Paris à Rouen n'a pas été long parce qu'il a passé le temps à (*in*) regarder la campagne. Il a remarqué (*noticed*) que les champs en France ne sont pas séparés l'un de l'autre par des haies (*hedges*) et que les femmes et les jeunes filles aident les hommes à cultiver des légumes ou à garder les moutons.

Quand ils arrivent à l'Hôtel Moderne, situé au centre de

la ville, l'employé au bureau (*office*) dit à M. Lebrun qu'il lui a réservé deux chambres à deux lits et il les invite à entrer dans l'ascenseur (*lift*). En réponse à une question Mme Lebrun annonce qu'elle trouve sa chambre très jolie. "Et vous, Jean?" "Ah, pour moi, les repas ont plus d'importance que les chambres!" "Il est une heure," dit M. Lebrun. "Allons au restaurant."

LESSON NINETEEN

HOW TO SAY "I HAVE SEEN THEM"

In Lesson Eleven we saw that when a past participle is used with any part of the verb "to be" the past participle must agree with the subject of the verb, just as an adjective agrees with its noun.

FOR example:

the door is high, *la porte est haute* (adjective)
the door is shut, *la porte est fermée* (participle)

Fermé is the Past Participle of *fermer* to shut, but here it is feminine (*fermée*) because it is used with *est* and agrees with *la porte*.

In "he has shut the door" we put *il a fermé la porte* because here the participle is used with *a* not *est*.

It is true that a Past Participle when used with any part of *avoir* (to have) does not change to agree with the subject of the sentence, but that is not the whole story. There are times when a Past Participle used with, say, *a* or *avait* does become feminine or plural, and it is very important to know when this happens.

"I saw (have seen) the man" is, of course, *J'ai vu l'homme*. In that sentence "I" is the subject. ("Who saw?" Answer "I") and "the man" is the object ("Saw whom?" Answer "the man").

In the sentence "I saw him" "I" is again the subject, and the object is this time "him" ("Saw whom?" Answer "Him"), and we should put *je l'ai vu*, because the pronoun object "him" must come before the verb.

Now look at these two:

I saw the woman. *J'ai vu la femme.*
I saw her. *Je l'ai vue.*

In each the object is feminine, in the first the noun *la femme*, in the second the pronoun *la* (or *l'*). There doesn't seem

75

much difference, yet in the first sentence we have *vu* and in the second *vue*. WHY? THE REASON is that in the first case the object *la femme* comes AFTER the verb, but in the second the object, being a pronoun, comes BEFORE the verb.

THIS GIVES US OUR RULE: A Past Participle used with any tense of *avoir* (to have) agrees with its DIRECT OBJECT *if* BUT ONLY *if that object is placed* BEFORE *the verb*.

Let's take one or two other sentences:

Where did you buy those shoes? *Où avez-vous acheté ces souliers?* (Object after verb so no agreement.)

I bought them at Dupont's. *Je les ai achetés chez Dupont.* (Object before verb, so Participle agrees.)

I gave her a bicycle. *Je lui ai donné une bicyclette.* (This means "gave a bicycle to her". *Une bicyclette* is the DIRECT OBJECT and *lui*, although coming before the verb, is only the indirect object, and therefore the Participle does not change.)

Have you seen them? *Les avez-vous vus?*

Haven't you seen them? *Ne les avez-vous pas vus?* (In both the direct object is *les* placed before the verb. The fact that there is a *ne . . . pas* in one sentence makes no difference. In each case we must put *vus*.)

Here are further examples:

Leur avez-vous parlé?—Did you speak to them? (No agreement because *leur* is not the direct object.)

Où sont mes livres? Je les ai perdus. Here *les* which refers to *livres* is the direct object, so *perdus* is plural. But in *je ne lui ai pas montré les journaux, lui* is the indirect, not the direct object, of *montré*.

Word List 19

le soulier, shoe	*la bicyclette*, bicycle
perdu, lost	*lu*, read

Exercise 19 (*a*)

Put into English:

1. Mme Leroux n'était pas chez elle, mais je l'ai rencontrée devant l'église. 2. Où sont les cartes-postales qui étaient sur cette table? Je les ai données au petit fils du médecin. 3. Je désirais du poisson mais le marchand nous a

envoyé de la viande. 4. Mes journaux ne sont pas ici. Les avez-vous prêtés à quelqu'un? 5. Je cherche ma bicyclette et je ne la trouve pas. Je suis sûr que quelqu'un l'a prise. 6. Les soldats marchaient au château et nous les avons regardés longtemps. 7. Cet auteur a écrit beaucoup de livres, mais je ne les ai pas lus. 8. Ce vieux monsieur et sa femme demeurent près de nous. Je les ai vus mais je ne leur ai jamais parlé. 9. Où sont vos amis? Ne les avez-vous pas vus? 10. Ma tante est très fâchée. Elle a acheté hier des fleurs et mon chien les a mangées. 11. Si vous n'aimez pas cette dame, pourquoi l'avez-vous invitée à dîner? 12. Avez-vous vu mes souliers? Les avez-vous perdus? Les chercherais-je, si je les avais trouvés?

Exercise 19 (b)

Put into French:

1. At what time did you meet your aunt? I met her in the street at four o'clock. 2. Those shoes are very big. Where did you buy them? 3. Mme Leroux is very angry because someone has sent her some old fish. 4. I sent it to Mme Leroux because I do not like her. 5. Your uncle and (your) aunt are in Paris. Have you written to them? 6. Where is your bicycle? I have put it behind a tree in the garden.

7. Where are the flowers which were in my room? I have lost them. 8. Why have you not invited your cousins to dinner? I have not invited them because they did not give us any presents. 9. I found some interesting books in that shop near the church. 10. I did not buy them because I hadn't enough money. 11. We used to have a car when we lived in the country, but we have sold it. 12. Are you sure that the door is shut? Yes, I shut it at eight o'clock.

Have a Try 19

A l'école Charles a eu des leçons d'histoire et son professeur lui a parlé de la vie de Jeanne d'Arc. Dans son livre d'histoire aussi Charles a lu avec intérêt de cette jeune fille qui sous l'inspiration des saints qui lui ont parlé a renoncé à (*given up*) là vie tranquille de son village de Domrémy pour aller sauver la France, désolée par l'invasion anglaise. Elle force les Anglais à abandonner le siège d'Orléans, mais bientôt après cette victoire elle tombe entre les mains des Bourguignons (*Burgundians*) qui la livrent (*hand over*) pour une immense somme d'argent à leurs alliés, les Anglais.

Après leur déjeuner à l'Hôtel Moderne Charles et Jean ont visité la tour (*tower*) où Jeanne d'Arc était prisonnière et la Place du Vieux Marché où elle a été brûlée (*burnt*).

LESSON TWENTY

HOW TO SAY "I HAD GIVEN"

We know that *j'avais* (the Imperfect of *avoir*) means "I had", though it can also mean "I was having" or "I used to have". Now, just as we can take the Present *j'ai* and follow it by a Past Participle *j'ai donné* to mean "I have given" (or "I gave"), so we can use *j'avais* (I had) with *donné* (given). Thus *j'avais donné*, I had given. *Nous avions parlé* we had spoken, or *ils avaient vu*, they had seen, and so on.

In the same way, just as we can use the Present of "to be" with a Past Participle *je suis caché*, I am hidden, so we can also use the Imperfect of "to be" with a Past Participle: *l'argent était caché*, the money was hidden.

We must, of course, remember, that if it is used with any tense of *être* (to be) the participle agrees with the subject of the verb just as an adjective does.

The door was shut. *La porte était fermée.*
Had you shut the door? *Aviez-vous fermé la porte?*
Yes, I had shut it. *Oui, je l'avais fermée.* (Participle is feminine because it is used with a part of *avoir* and must agree with the object pronoun which comes in front of it.)

How to Say "This one" or "That one"

We know already how to put "this", "that", "these" or "those" into French when each of these words is followed by a noun.

ce chapeau, this hat; *cet homme*, this man; *cette vache*, this cow; *ces soldats* (*maisons*), these soldiers (houses)

We know, too, that if we want to distinguish between "this" and "that" we can do so by putting -*ci* (short for *ici*—here) or -*là* (there) after the noun.

This book belongs to me, but that book belongs to him. *Ce livre-ci est à moi, mais ce livre-là est à lui.*

BUT SURELY, in English, we should be much more likely to
say "This book belongs to me, but that one belongs to
him"? In other words, we want to know the French for
"this" (one) without having to repeat the noun "book".
We can do it like this:

"This (that) one" standing for a masculine noun is *celui*.
"This (that) one" standing for a feminine noun is *celle*.
"These (those) ones" standing for a masculine noun is *ceux*.
"These (those) ones" standing for a feminine noun is *celles*.

Examples:

This book belongs to me, that one belongs to him. *Ce livre-ci est à
moi, celui-là est à lui.*
My house is the one which has a green door. *Ma maison est celle qui
a une porte verte.*
Those men are soldiers, these are policemen. *Ces hommes-là sont
des soldats: ceux-ci sont des agents de police.*

Word List 20

une personne, a person	*jeter*, to throw
des personnes, some people	*reçu*, received
une brique, a brick	*que*, than

Exercise 20 (*a*)

Put into English:

1. Mon cousin désirait acheter ma vieille bicyclette, mais
je l'avais vendue déjà. 2. J'étais sûr que quelqu'un avait pris
mes souliers, parce que je les ai cherchés dans toutes les
chambres. 3. Le marchand était très fâché parce que de
méchants garçons avaient jeté des briques dans la rue.
4. Ils avaient cassé douze bouteilles de bière qu'il allait
envoyer à l'hôtel. 5. Je vous ai dit que ces souliers-ci sont
à moi: ceux-là sont au monsieur qui est assis à la table près
de la fenêtre. 6. J'ai acheté ce livre-ci parce qu'il est plus
intéressant que celui-là. 7. Il y a dix personnes dans cette
voiture: montons dans celle-ci, où nous trouverons des
places libres. 8. Nous avons visité beaucoup de châteaux,
mais nous préférons celui-ci parce qu'il est plus beau que

tous les autres. 9. Quel tableau préférez-vous? Celui-ci ou celui que je vous ai apporté? 10. Nous n'étions pas sûrs dans quel train vous arriveriez—le train de deux heures ou celui que vous avez pris hier. 11. La bicyclette verte n'est pas à moi, mais je vous prêterai celle-ci. 12. Où sont vos souliers? Je les ai perdus: mon cousin m'a donné ceux-ci.

Exercise 20 (b)

Put into French:

1. Who was that lady? Which lady? That one who was looking at the flowers. 2. In which house used you to live? In that one. It has a nice garden, but the rooms were very small. 3. Of these two books, we prefer this one, because I have read the other. 4. Let us get into (*monter*) this carriage: there are two dogs and five children in that one. 5. I was sure that I had never seen that old lady. But this one, who is crossing the road, is a friend of my aunt. 6. This is the window which is broken. Look at it! 7. Had you not read in the newspaper that the queen was going to spend a week at the castle? 8. Which castle? The (that) one, which I showed you when we made an excursion. 9. There are fifty people in this hotel and all the tables are occupied. No, this

one is free. 10. I told (said to) my sister that I had written
her a long letter, but she has not received it. 11. These cows
and those belong to my uncle. We used to have some cows
but we have sold them. 12. Are you the naughty little boy
who threw this brick? No, madam. I threw that one.

Have a Try 20

Charles, qui était fatigué, a passé une bonne nuit. Jean et
sa mère sont déjà dans la salle à manger de l'hôtel et
Charles arrive au moment où le garçon apporte le petit
déjeuner qui consiste en (*of*) une bonne tasse de café ou de
chocolat avec du pain et du beurre normand. C'est un repas
moins substantiel que le petit déjeuner anglais, mais en
France on (*one*) a le déjeuner une heure plus tôt qu' (*earlier
than*) en Angleterre.

LESSON TWENTY-ONE

THE USE OF C'EST

We know that *il est* means "he is" and sometimes "it is". For instance, "it is certain that he is not here", *il est certain qu'il n'est pas ici.* But in French "it is" is frequently translated as *c'est.* This happens, for instance, when "it is" is followed by a personal pronoun.

It is you whom I saw. *C'est vous que j'ai vu.*

REMEMBER that *je* can be used only as the subject of a verb. If there is no verb we must use *moi*: just as we do after a preposition—*avec moi*, with me (see Lesson Twelve) so:

it is I, *c'est moi*   it is he, *c'est lui*

BUT *c'est* can also be used followed by a noun, and in this case it can mean, if necessary, "he (she) is".

Who is at the door? It is a man whom I have never seen. *Qui est à la porte? C'est un homme que je n'ai jamais vu.*

He is an extraordinary man! *C'est un homme extraordinaire!* (*C'est* is turned into *est-ce* in questions.)

Who is there? Is it you, Charles? Yes, it is I. *Qui est là? Est-ce vous, Charles? Oui, c'est moi.* (*C'est* can be used followed by an adjective, but the "it" usually refers to something already mentioned.)

Have you done your work? Yes, it isn't difficult. *Avez-vous fait votre travail? Oui, ce n'est pas difficile.*

How to Say "I shall have" and "I should have"

We know already (Lesson Twelve) that the Future Tenses of all verbs have the same ending: *-ai, -as, -a, -ons, -ez* and *-ont.* Usually we can get the Future by adding these endings to the Infinitive of the verb: *je donnerai, je trouverai* and so on. BUT there are a few verbs which don't follow this rule. Among these is *avoir.* Here is its Future:

j'aurai, I shall have	*nous aurons*, we shall have
(*tu auras*)	*vous aurez*, you will have
il aura, he will have	*ils auront*, they will have

In the same way, we know that the Conditional (I should) of every verb ends in: *-ais, -ais, -ait, -ions, -iez, -aient.* Usually we form the Conditional by adding these endings to the Infinitive: *je donnerais, je trouverais.*

AGAIN, there are exceptions. One of them is *avoir* and to get the Conditional we alter it in exactly the same way as we did when forming the Future.

j'aurais, I should have   *nous aurions*, we should have
(tu aurais)   *vous auriez*, you would have
il aurait, he would have   *ils auraient*, they would have

Word List 21

su, known   *le moment*, the moment   *vite*, quickly

Exercise 21 (*a*)

Put into English:

1. Je n'ai pas pris vos dix francs: c'est cet enfant-là qui les a trouvés. 2. Si j'avais su que vos amis allaient arriver par le train de dix heures je les aurais rencontrés à la gare. 3. Si vous me prêtez deux francs j'aurai assez d'argent pour acheter du poisson et des fruits pour le déjeuner. 4. Qui est ce monsieur? C'est l'oncle de Jean. C'est lui qui a acheté notre vieille voiture. 5. Qui est ce jeune homme-là? Celui-là? C'est un touriste américain. 6. Quel livre achetez-vous? C'est un livre de l'auteur que nous avons rencontré chez M. Leriche. C'est très intéressant. 7. Regardez ces arbres-là. Nous aurons de belles pommes. 8. J'aurais eu de beaux fruits dans mon jardin, si votre petit neveu ne les avait pas volés. 9. Je n'aime pas ce monsieur. C'est lui qui a fermé la porte du compartiment au moment où (*when*) je désirais monter dans le train. 10. Est-ce derrière cet arbre-ci que vous avez mis votre bicyclette? 11. Je vous aurais écrit si j'avais su dans quel hôtel vous passiez vos vacances. 12. Ma tante ne voyage jamais en avion: elle pense que c'est dangereux.

Exercise 21 (*b*)

Put into French:

1. Of these two pictures it is this one that we prefer.
2. Have you enough money (in order) to buy some vegetables? 3. Did you see that young lady? She is the daughter
of our neighbour. 4. If I had known at what time (*heure*)
your train would arrive I would not have walked so quickly
to the station. 5. It is not at this hotel, but at that one, that
we shall meet you tomorrow. 6. Is it he, or his sister, who
(has) won all the prizes? 7. He is an extraordinary man. He
has an aeroplane and two big cars, but he travels always by
(*à*) bicycle. 8. Tomorrow for our breakfast we shall have
cups of coffee with some bread and (some) butter. 9. Do not
let us get into that compartment. In this one there are four
places which are vacant. 10. Do not walk so near the water.
It's dangerous. 11. He is an excellent doctor, but we don't
like him much. 12. I shall not work in this factory. I should
have too much work.

Have a Try 21

Pendant que M. Lebrun visite un client, Jean et Charles
sont en promenade (*on a walk*) dans la ville. Mme Lebrun a
prêté son guide à son fils et Charles a acheté un plan de
Rouen. Ils arrivent sans difficulté à la Place Notre Dame,
où est située la cathédrale. "Regardez ces deux grandes
tours," dit Jean. "Celle-ci est La Tour St. Romain, celle-là
est la Tour de Beurre." "De Beurre! Pourquoi? C'est
extraordinaire." Jean consulte son guide. "Ah, oui. Le
monsieur qui a écrit ce livre nous donne l'explication. Dans
le bon vieux temps (*plural in English*) il (*it*) était défendu
(*forbidden*) aux Catholiques de manger du beurre en Carême
(*Lent*), mais l'évêque (*bishop*) a déclaré que les personnes
qui lui donneraient de l'argent pour la construction de cette
Tour auraient sa permission de (*to*) manger du beurre en

Carême." "C'est très intéressant," dit Charles, "mais si je donnais mon argent cette tour aurait reçu le nom (*name*) de la Tour de Chocolat!"

LESSON TWENTY-TWO

HOW TO TELL THE TIME IN FRENCH

There are three words which mean "time" in French, and we must distinguish between them.

Fois (fem.) means "time" in the sense of "once", "twice", "three times".

une fois, deux fois, trois fois and so on.

Temps (masc.) means "time" in a general sense.

longtemps, (for) a long time
Le temps passait vite. The time was quickly passing. (It also means "weather".)
Le temps était beau. The weather was fine.

Heure (fem.) means the "time of day", "o'clock" or "hour".

Il est trois heures. It is three o'clock.
Quelle heure est-il? What time is it?
Je l'ai cherché pendant trois heures. I looked for him for three hours.

The French for "minute" is *minute* (fem.), but the simplest method is to leave it out.

From the hour up to half-past the hour we have only to give the hour, and follow this with the number of minutes so:

ten minutes past three, *trois heures dix*
twenty-five minutes past ten, *dix heures vingt-cinq*

For "a quarter-past one" we could in the same way put *une heure quinze*, but we could put instead *une heure et quart*, one o'clock and quarter.

For "half-past two" we could put *deux heures trente* (2.30), but there is also *deux heures et demie*. *Demi(e)* means "half" and is made feminine because "half" here means "half (an hour)" and *heure* is a feminine noun.

From the half hour until the next hour, we use *moins*, less. When in English we say "twenty minutes to two" the French

method is to turn this into "two hours less (or 'minus')
twenty": *deux heures moins vingt*. SIMILARLY "five minutes
to three" becomes "three hours less five"—*trois heures
moins cinq*.

For "twelve o'clock" it is usual to use *midi* (midday) and
minuit (midnight).

Il est midi dix. It is ten minutes past twelve.
Il est minuit moins dix. It is ten minutes to twelve (at night).

IN ENGLISH we say "three o'clock IN the afternoon" or
"eleven AT night". The French use *de* NOT *dans*.

trois heures de l'après-midi; onze heures de la nuit

How to Say "I shall be" and "I should be"

Just as "I shall have" is *j'aurai* and "I should have" is
j'aurais, the verb *être* (to be) is exceptional in the Future and
Conditional. Instead of adding the vowel endings to the
Infinitive we put *ser* instead of *être* and then add the endings.

je serai, I shall be	*je serais*, I should be
(tu seras)	*(tu serais)*
il sera	*il serait*
nous serons	*nous serions*
vous serez	*vous seriez*
ils seront	*ils seraient*

Word List 22

la représentation, the performance	*pardon*, excuse me
le théâtre, theatre	*s'il vous plaît*, please
aimable, kind, amiable	*merci*, thank you
le soir, the evening	*le chocolat*, chocolate
commencer, to begin	*Angleterre* (fem.), England

Exercise 22 (a)

Put into English:

1. Je vous ai dit deux fois que je serai au marché à deux
heures et demie si le temps est beau. 2. Marchons vite,
nous n'avons pas beaucoup de temps. Il est déjà trois

heures moins vingt (*minutes*). 3. La représentation commencera à huit heures du soir, mais je vous rencontrerai
devant le théâtre à sept heures et quart. 4. Pardon, monsieur, quelle heure est-il, s'il vous plaît? 5. Il est neuf
heures moins quinze, madame. Merci, monsieur. 6. Cette
jeune fille est très aimable. J'allais monter dans ce train-là,
mais elle m'a dit que notre train ne sera pas ici avant onze
heures vingt-cinq. 7. Il est deux heures moins cinq à (*by*)
ma montre. Nous aurons le temps d' (*to*) acheter des journaux et des cartes postales. 8. Marchez plus vite, s'il vous
plaît. Il sera déjà minuit quand nous arriverons[1] chez nous.
9. En Angleterre nous avons le déjeuner à une heure, mais si
vous passez vos vacances en France vous aurez le déjeuner
à midi. 10. Si vous montez dans ce train vous serez à Paris
à six heures et quart. 11. Je les aurais rencontrés si j'avais
su à quelle heure ils seraient à la gare. 12. Est-il déjà midi?
Non, il est onze heures et demie.

Exercise 22 (*b*)

Put into French:

1. It is half-past three. I thought (that) she would be here
before two o'clock. 2. I have seen her twice, but I have never
spoken to her. 3. At what time will you be at the station?
At a quarter to four. 4. The performance will not begin
before half-past eight in (of) the evening. 5. If we arrive at
the theatre at twenty minutes to eight we shall have the time
to (*d'*) buy some fruit and some chocolate. 6. Excuse me,
sir, what time is it, please? It is twenty-past ten, madam.
7. We shall not have enough time (in order) to visit the
castle. It is already ten minutes to twelve (midday). 8. We
shall not be home before midnight if we do not walk more
quickly. 9. What time was it when you saw her yesterday?
It was ten minutes to six. 10. I thought that the shops would

[1] In English "we arrive", but the sense is really "will arrive", and
with *quand* in such cases the French use the Future not the Present.

be shut, because it was already half-past five. 11. How many times have you been to Paris? Three or four times. It's a lovely city (town). 12. How much time did you spend at the doctor's (house)? We were at his house from three o'clock until a quarter to four.

Have a Try 22

A onze heures et quart, Mme Lebrun et les deux garçons sont au bord de la mer. Après le petit déjeuner ils ont marché à la gare où ils ont pris le rapide (*express*) qui les a amenés (*brought*) en très peu de temps à Dieppe. Là ils montent dans un des autobus qui assurent le service entre Dieppe et le Tréport et ils descendent de l'autobus à une jolie petite plage (*beach*).

Jean et Charles regardent avec satisfaction l'eau claire et calme. En cinq minutes ils sont en maillot (*bathing-dress*).

Jean indique un rocher (*rock*) qui perce (*pierces*) la surface de l'eau à une distance de trente mètres (*yards, metres*).

"Je gage (*bet*) que j'arriverai à ce rocher avant vous," dit-il.

Les deux garçons commencent à nager (*swim*) de toutes leurs forces. La tête plongée dans l'eau, Charles ne remarque pas un vieux monsieur devant lui et entre en collision violente avec lui. Quand il lui a fait ses excuses Jean est assis déjà sur le rocher.

LESSON TWENTY-THREE

HOW TO SAY "I HAVE COME"

Now and then, in the Bible or even in modern books, we may come across phrases such as "he is gone" or "the time is come", instead of the usual "has gone" or "has come".

Anyway, the point is that there are certain verbs in French where we have to use, say, *est* not *a* before the Past Participle. Most of these, though not all, are verbs of motion, that is to do with coming, going, falling and so on.

HERE are the Past Participles of some of these verbs with which we must remember to use, for instance, *je suis*, and not *j'ai*, even though the English is "I have" not "I am".

Some of them we know already.

allé, gone
parti, departed, set out (for)
monté, gone up, got into
descendu, gone down, descended
devenu, become
arrivé, arrived

tombé, fallen
venu, come
revenu, come back
entré, entered, went into
resté, remained

We must remember, too, that if we use *est* not *a* before a Past Participle the participle must agree, like an adjective, with the subject of the verb. The following examples will show what we have to do:

He has shut the door. *Il a fermé la porte.*
The door is shut. *La porte est fermée.*

In the first we use *a* because the verb is not one of the ones in the list above. In the second we naturally use *est* because the English is "is".

BUT:

He has gone (*or* he went) to the pictures. *Il est allé au cinéma.*
They arrived at the station. *Ils sont arrivés à la gare.*

In the same way, of course, we must use *était* not *avait* for "had" before these same participles.

I had not seen her. *Je ne l'avais pas vue.*
She had fallen into the water. *Elle était tombée dans l'eau.*
She would have fallen. *Elle serait tombée.*

How to Say "First", "Second" and so on

We know already the French numbers, one, two, three up to sixty or so. We need also to be able to say "the first" "the second" and so on.

The French for "first" is *premier*. This is an adjective and its feminine, like those of other words ending in *-er*, is formed by changing this into *-ère*: *cher* (dear)—*chère*; *le premier—la première*.

IN ENGLISH we usually add "th" to the number—"seventh", "nine"—"ninth", dropping the final "e" (if there is one) before adding the "th".

IN FRENCH, in the same way, we add *-ième*: *trois—le (la) troisième*, third; *quatre—le (la) quatrième*, fourth.

In numbers from 17 upwards, when the number is made up of two words, we add *-ième* to the second only: 20th, *le vingtième*; 21st, *le vingt et unième*; 22nd, *le vingt-deuxième*.

There is no need to give a list of all the numbers. But here are a few, including those in which a slight alteration in spelling is made in changing the (cardinal) number into the ordinal (that is one which indicates the order, 3rd, 4th, 5th).

first, *le premier (la première)*   eleventh, *le (la) onzième*[2]
second, *le (la) deuxième*   seventeenth, *le (la) dix-septième*
fifth, *le (la) cinquième*   fifty-fifth, *le cinquante-cinquième*
ninth, *le (la) neuvième*[1]

Word List 23

un étage, a floor   *la cave*, cellar   *la clef*,[3] key

---

[1] NOTE that the "f" of *neuf* is softened into a "v" (*neuvième*), as with "hoof", "hooves" in English.

[2] By exception le (la) is NOT shortened into *l'* before *onze* or *onzième*.

[3] Pronounced rather like "clay" in English.

Exercise 23 (*a*)

Put into English:

1. Non, monsieur, Mme Dupont n'est pas chez elle. Elle est partie ce matin pour la campagne. 2. Si ces petits garçons n'étaient pas montés dans ce mauvais petit bateau ils ne seraient pas tombés dans l'eau. 3. Hier nous sommes allés à Paris pour la première fois. 4. Notre hôtel est très grand. Nous avons une belle chambre au quatrième étage. 5. Elle allait passer ses vacances au bord de la mer, mais elle est revenue à Paris après cinq jours. 6. A l'école elle était toujours la première de sa classe, mais elle est devenue très paresseuse. 7. Nous avons fait une belle excursion, mais ma tante, qui était malade, est restée à l'hôtel. 8. Le propriétaire est descendu à la cave pour chercher une bouteille de vin blanc. 9. Si vous aviez marché plus vite, nous serions arrivés chez nous à l'heure du déjeuner. 10. Quand je suis arrivé chez M. Dubois, sa sœur m'a dit qu'il était parti déjà pour Bordeaux. 11. C'est le dixième jour de nos vacances. C'est aussi le neuvième jour de mauvais temps! 12. Elle ne nous a pas dit qu'elle était revenue par avion.

Exercise 23 (*b*)

Put into French:

1. At what time did she arrive at your house? At midnight. 2. I had gone up to my room on the seventh floor. 3. He has gone to Paris, but his sister has remained at home. 4. We went into the hotel, but our friends had departed already for the seaside. 5. We live in the first house in (of) the street. It has a green door. 6. I have bought three tickets for the second performance of this evening. It begins at half-past eight. 7. We would not have come back if we had known that you were not at home (use *chez*). 8. When we arrived at the station, the train had already left (departed). 9. The police went down to the cellar, where they

found two young thieves who were hidden behind the bottles. 10. Mme Dupont is very angry. She went up as far as the ninth floor and on (*en*) arriving at her door she found that she had lost her key. 11. When I saw her for the first time she was young. Now she has become very old. 12. When did they return (have they returned) from the seaside? They arrived home (use *chez*) yesterday at half-past seven.

Have a Try 23

A Paris il y a beaucoup de maisons qui n'ont pas d'ascenseur. Pour cette raison une personne qui occupe un appartement (*flat*) au premier étage est en général dans la nécessité de payer un loyer (*rent*) plus considérable que le locataire (*tenant, occupant*) d'un appartement au sixième.

M. Billot n'était pas riche et c'est pourquoi l'appartement où il passait sa vieillesse était au septième étage. Le vieux monsieur avait dans sa chambre une horloge de parquet (*grandfather clock*). Un jour il a remarqué avec regret que cette horloge qu'il aimait beaucoup ne marchait pas bien. Un horloger est venu emporter (*take away, carry off*) l'horloge pour la réparer.

Cinq jours après un homme est descendu d'une voiture de livraison (*delivery*) devant la maison et a commencé à

monter l'escalier, en portant l'horloge qui était maintenant
en bon état (*state*, *condition*). A ce moment un jeune homme,
qui demeurait aussi dans la maison, a vu le porteur qui
montait avec difficulté parce que la grande horloge était
très lourde (*heavy*). "Mon ami," lui dit-il d'un air innocent.
"Si vous désirez savoir (*know*) l'heure, pourquoi ne portez-
vous pas une montre? Ce serait beaucoup plus simple!"

LESSON TWENTY-FOUR

HOW TO SAY "WHICH ONE?" OR "WHICH OF?"

We know that "this" before a noun is *ce, cet* or *cette* and that "this one" (Lesson Twenty) is *celui* or *celle*.

cette maison; ma maison est celle-ci

We also know that "which (what)" followed by a noun is *quel(s)* (masc.) or *quelle(s)* (fem.).

Quelle heure est-il? What time is it?

BUT how are we to say "which one, etc."?

For this we use *lequel*, and as it is made up of the article *le* and *quel*, it can, although written in one word, have the following forms: *lequel, laquelle, lesquels* and *lesquelles*.

We can even have *duquel, de laquelle, desquel(le)s* or *auquel, à laquelle* and *auxquel(le)s*, but we need not bother about most of these here.

REMEMBER that *quel* is used with a noun, while *lequel* stands instead of one (just as with *ce* and *celui*).

Quels livres avez-vous pris? Which books have you taken?
Lequel de ces deux livres avez-vous acheté? Which of these two books have you bought?
Dans quelle maison est-il entré? Into which house did he go?
Dans laquelle de ces maisons est-il entré? Into which of these houses did he go?
Auquel de ces deux garçons avez-vous prêté ma bicyclette? To which of these two boys did you lend my bicycle?

How to Say "Bigger" and "Biggest"

When we use words such as "bigger" we are using what is called the "comparative", because something is bigger (or smaller) than or in comparison with something else. We can say "larger" or "thinner", but not, for instance, "interest-inger" or "intelligenter". Instead we say, of course, "more

97

interesting", "more intelligent". In French we use *plus* (more) not only with longer words such as *intéressant* but with short ones such as *grand* or *vieux*.

> My car is bigger than that one. *Ma voiture est plus grande que celle-là.*

SOMETIMES the French will use *moins* (less) in the same way.

> He is less intelligent (more stupid) than his brother. *Il est moins intelligent (plus bête) que son frère.*

BUT there are a few adjectives which have a special comparative form in French. Just as we say "better" NOT "more good", so the French say *meilleur* NOT *plus bon*.

> *Ces livres sont meilleurs que ceux-là.* These books are better than those.

If we want to say "biggest" in French, all we have to do is to put *le* (*la, les*) before the French for "bigger".

> *plus grand* becomes *le plus grand*
> *la plus grande maison*, the biggest house

It follows that as *meilleur* is "better", "best" is *le meilleur* (WITHOUT *plus*).

> *les meilleurs hôtels*, the best hotels

Exercise 24 (a)

Put into English:

1. Laquelle de ces deux bicyclettes est à vous? Celle-ci est à moi. 2. Le monsieur à qui j'ai vendu ma voiture est parti pour la campagne. 3. Auquel de ces messieurs avez-vous prêté mon journal? A celui-là. 4. Le couteau avec lequel vous avez coupé le pain est meilleur que celui-ci. 5. Les chambres au cinquième étage sont plus petites que celles du premier, mais elles sont moins chères. 6. De tous les hôtels de cette ville l'Hôtel de la Gare est le plus grand, mais au Cheval Blanc les repas sont meilleurs. 7. Mme Chose est plus jeune que ma tante, mais elle est beaucoup moins aimable. 8. Il y a cinquante-cinq chambres dans cet

hôtel. Laquelle est celle de vos amis? 9. Cet auteur a écrit beaucoup de livres. Lequel préferez-vous? 10. Le propriétaire m'a donné deux clefs. Laquelle est celle de votre chambre? 11. J'ai vu un voleur qui entrait par une fenêtre dans une de ces maisons: mais laquelle? 12. Notre voisin est plus riche que nous: il voyage en première classe et dans les hôtels il a toujours la meilleure chambre.

Exercise 24 (b)

Put into French:

1. We have two rooms which are free. Which do you prefer? 2. Into which of these two rooms have you put my suitcase? Into that one, madam. 3. To which of these girls did you give my key? 4. To which of these two boys did you lend my knife? 5. The castle which we visited yesterday is bigger than this one. 6. If you go to the Station Hotel you will have a nice room, but the meals here are much better. 7. We have sold the house in which we used to live. 8. There are many cafés in this town. Into which did he go? 9. The horse is cleverer than the sheep, but the elephant is the most intelligent of all the animals. 10. Of which man were you speaking? Of the doctor. 11. Of which of these two gentlemen were you speaking? Of that one. 12. The town to which he has gone is near the sea.

Have a Try 24

"Où allez-vous passer vos vacances, mon ami?" "A Paris. Ce sera ma première visite." "En ce cas (*case*) je vous conseille (*advise*) de loger dans un hôtel près de la Place St. Michel." "Pourquoi?" "Parce que dans cette partie de la ville il y a des hôtels où vous trouverez tout le confort que vous désirez à un prix raisonnable." "Oui, mais je serais à une distance considérable du centre de Paris et si je suis forcé de monter dans un taxi pour aller à la Cathédrale, au Louvre ou aux grands magasins, je n'aurai pas assez d'argent pour payer ma chambre à l'hôtel ou mes repas dans un restaurant." "Mais non, il y a un excellent service d'autobus et vous avez aussi le Métropolitain" (*Underground*).

LESSON TWENTY-FIVE

ABOUT "MYSELF"

We know that when a pronoun is the object of a verb it must come before that verb.

Thus "the thief hides his money", *le voleur cache son argent*, but "he hides it" is *il le cache*. Now *il le cache* might also mean "he hides him", as for instance, when someone helps an escaping prisoner by concealing him from his pursuers. The *il* refers to one person, the *le* to another. But the escaping prisoner might, for instance, seek to throw his pursuers off the scent by his own efforts. He might think, "I will hide myself behind that tree" (while they go by). In "I hide him" the subject "I" represents one person and "him" another: *je le cache*. But in "I hide myself" the subject "I" and the object "myself" are both the same person, namely, "me". We therefore put *je me cache*. "We hide ourselves" would be *nous nous cachons*. But how are we to say "he hides himself"? We can't put *il le cache*, because that means that "he (one person) hides him (somebody else)". So in the third person we have to use a new object pronoun *se*. This can mean either "himself", "herself", "themselves" or, with the Infinitive, "oneself". Thus *se cacher* is "to hide oneself", and its Present Tense, in full, would be:

Je me cache, I hide myself	*nous nous cachons*, we hide ourselves.
(tu te caches)	*vous vous cachez*
il (elle) se cache	*ils se cachent*

We can use *se* also as the indirect object of a verb. For instance, "I will give him a present". This really means "I will give a present (direct object) to him (indirect object)" *Je lui donnerai un cadeau*. But you can buy presents for yourself as well as other people. So we can put:

I will give myself a present. *Je me donnerai un cadeau.*

and

She will give herself a present. *Elle se donnera un cadeau.*

SOMETIMES a French verb must be used with an object when we can leave it out in English. For instance "That small boy never washes (himself)". In French the *se* must be put in: *Ce petit garçon ne se lave jamais*. Again, *arrêter* means "to arrest", but *s'arrêter* means "to stop".

The policeman arrests the thief. *L'agent de police arrête le voleur.*
The train does not stop here. *Le train ne s'arrête pas ici.*

Days and Months

HERE are the days of the week:

(*le*) *dimanche*, Sunday	(*le*) *jeudi*, Thursday
(*le*) *lundi*, Monday	(*le*) *vendredi*, Friday
(*le*) *mardi*, Tuesday	(*le*) *samedi*, Saturday
(*le*) *mercredi*, Wednesday	

HERE are the months of the year:

(*le*) *janvier*, January	(*l'*) *août*, August
(*le*) *février*, February	(*le*) *septembre*, September
(*le*) *mars*, March	(*l'*) *octobre*, October
(*l'*) *avril*, April	(*le*) *novembre*, November
(*le*) *mai*, May	(*le*) *décembre*, December
(*le*) *juin*, June	*le mois*, month
(*le*)*juillet*, July	

Here, just as a matter of interest, is the French for certain special days:

Le jour de l'an, New Year's Day
(*Le*) *mardi gras*, Shrove Tuesday
(*Le*) *mercredi des Cendres*, Ash Wednesday
(*Le*) *dimanche de Pâques*, Easter Sunday
(*Le*) *Noël*, Christmas
La veille de Noël, Christmas Eve

NOTE

(1) Days and months are written in French with a small NOT a capital letter.

(2) In dates use *premier* for the 1st of the month, but *deux*, *trois* and so on for all the others.

(3) Do not translate "on" before days of the week or "of" in dates of the months.

on Monday, the first of July, *lundi le premier juillet*
on Wednesday, the ninth of April, *mercredi le neuf avril*

THERE is no need to learn all these days and months at once: turn to the list and after a while you will find that you know them.

Word List 25

(se) *blesser*, to wound (oneself)
s'habiller, to dress, get dressed
s'approcher(de), to approach, draw near (to)

la voie, (railway) track, line
prudent, prudent, careful
l'herbe (fem.), grass
jeter, to throw

Exercise 25 (a)

Put into English:

1. Le train s'arrête parce qu'une vieille vache est assise sur

la voie: il y a des voyageurs qui sont très fâchés   2. Lundi, le premier janvier nous sommes allés au théâtre. 3. Jeudi le vingt-huit juillet nous sommes partis par avion pour la France. 4. Ne traversez pas la voie au moment où un train s'approche. 5. Le chasseur n'a pas tué le tigre. Il l'a blessé et le pauvre animal se cache dans l'herbe. 6. Le cinq novembre les agents de police ont arrêté beacoup de personnes qui jetaient des pétards (*squibs*) dans la rue. 7. Si vous tombez dans cette eau profonde, vous vous tuerez. 8. Du vingt août jusqu'au six septembre je serai au bord de la mer avec mon père. 9. Quand êtes-vous revenus de Paris? Nous sommes arrivés chez nous samedi le trente juillet. 10. Si vous ne vous habillez pas vite, vous n'aurez pas de petit déjeuner. 11. Si nous nous cachons dans la cave ils ne nous trouveront pas. 12. Si vous n'êtes pas prudent vous vous blesserez. Ces grands couteaux-là sont dangereux.

Exercise 25 (b)

Put into French:

1. If the train does not stop at this little station we will walk as far as the town. 2. (On) Thursday we do not go to (the) school and our holidays will begin (on) the fifteenth of December. 3. If you throw those squibs (*pétards*) you will wound someone. 4. You will kill yourself if you are not careful. 5. A sheep has been killed, because it was crossing the line while the train was approaching. 6. I am sure that those boys have not gone to school. Where are they hiding? 7. The dog has hidden the fish in my aunt's bed. She will be very angry! 8. (On) Friday, the 13th (of) June we shall be in Paris. 9. We dress very quickly when we are at the seaside. 10. My sister departed for London on the first of April and she came back here on the second of May. 11. Excuse me, madame, the trains do not stop here. This station is shut. 12. She will wound herself if she is not careful.

Have a Try 25

"Vous m'avez dit qu'à Paris il est possible d'aller sans difficulté par autobus de la Place St. Michel, par exemple, jusqu'à la Place de l'Opéra!"

"Oui. C'est très simple et, si vous achetez un carnet (*booklet*) de billets, vous trouverez que ce sera moins cher que (*than*) d'acheter un billet chaque (*each*) fois que vous montez dans un autobus. Si vous allez par le Métropolitain, il est possible de changer de train une ou deux fois et votre billet reste valable (*valid, usable*) jusqu'au moment où vous montez à la surface.

come in front of the verb, but in what order? Which do we put first? Fortunately, it's quite simple. This is the rule. With two object pronouns, put the indirect before the direct *except when they are both third person.*

For instance: in "I will give it to you" "it" is the direct object and "to you" the indirect; "it" is 3rd Person and "to you" 2nd Person, so the indirect "to you" comes first: *je vous le donnerai.*

BUT in "I will give it to him" both "it" and "to him" are in the 3rd Person, so the direct object comes first: *je le lui donnerai.*

Whether the sentence is in the form of a question or has a "not" in it makes no difference: indirect before direct unless both are in the 3rd Person. Here are further examples:

He has sent it to us. *Il nous l'a envoyé.*
I have sent it to them. *Je le leur ai envoyé.*
Did you give it to him? *Le lui avez-vous donné?*
Didn't he give it to you? *Ne vous l'a-t-il pas donné?*

This last one looks a bit difficult, but it isn't really. The list in Lesson Twelve will give you the pronouns, if you're not sure of them, and the rule just given will tell you the order to put them in. Of course *me* and *nous* are in the 1st Person, *vous* is in the 2nd, and *le, la, les, lui* and *leur* are all in the 3rd Person.

Word List 26

un timbre-poste, (postage) stamp
des timbres-poste, (postage) stamps
la tasse, cup
descendre, to go down, descend, to stay (at a hotel)
rendre, to render, give back

Exercise 26 (*a*)

Put into English:

1. Pendant que je descendais l'escalier j'ai rencontré un touriste américain qui montait au quatrième étage. 2. Cette vieille femme vendait des fruits et des légumes au marché. 3. Ce vieux monsieur est très pauvre: si vous ne désirez pas

acheter ma vieille bicyclette je la lui donnerai. 4. Mon ami
ne vous prêtera pas sa voiture, parce qu'il me l'a vendue.
5. Ce monsieur est très fâché parce qu'il m'a prêté hier sa
valise et je ne la lui ai pas rendue. 6. Si vous ne me rendez
pas l'argent que vous avez volé les agents de police vous
arrêteront. 7. J'ai écrit une longue lettre à ma cousine,
mais je ne la lui ai pas envoyée. 8. Pourquoi? Parce que je
n'avais pas de timbres-poste. 9. Je vous prêterai un franc
pour acheter des timbres-poste, si vous me le rendez cet
après-midi. 10. Si vous descendez dans la cave vous trouverez des bouteilles de vin rouge qui est très bon. 11. Qui
vous les a données? C'est mon frère qui me les a données. Il
les a reçues d'un ami. 12. Si je n'avais pas vendu ma voiture
je vous l'aurais prêtée.

Exercise 26 (b)

Put into French:

1. I give him some money. 2. He sells me some stamps.
3. I give them to him. 4. He sells them to me. 5. I will give
it (*masc.*) to you. 6. We will give it (*fem.*) to her. 7. I will
show them to you. 8. We used to sell it (*fem.*) to them.
9. He has lent it (*masc.*) to us. 10. He has lent it (*fem.*) to
you. 11. I have not sent it (*masc.*) to her. 12. I have not
sent it (*fem.*) to them.

Exercise 26 (c)

Put into French:

1. If you go down to the dining-room you will find some
cups on the table. 2. I have lent him some money, but he has
not given it back to me. 3. Why has he not given it back to
you? 4. Someone has sold me some very good stamps.
5. I have an old bicycle. I shall lend it to you. 6. I shall not
lend it (*fem.*) to him. 7. Why will you not lend it (*fem.*) to
us? 8. If I had known that you had read this book I would
not have sent it to you. 9. They would have sent it to us.
10. Has he not given them (*masc. pl.*) back to you?

Have a Try 26

Un jour un fermier normand est allé visiter son voisin qui était marchand de charbon (*coal*). "Je suis venu vous demander un petit service," lui dit-il. "Quel service?" "C'est une question du charbon que je désire acheter." "Oui. Dans ces sacs-là il y a du charbon qui est très bon. Si par (*for*) exemple vous désirez dix sacs je vous les vends à dix francs le sac." "C'est assez cher," lui répond le fermier. "Le petit service duquel j'ai parlé, c'est que vous me vendez ce charbon à un prix réduit (*reduced*), parce que je suis un de vos meilleurs amis." "Vous me demandez quelque-chose d'exceptionnel," répond le marchand, "mais puisque (*since*) vous êtes mon ami je vous vends ce charbon à huit francs."

Le fermier est parti très content, mais un mois après il est revenu. "Ce charbon brûle (*burns*) très vite," dit-il. "Je parle du charbon que vous m'avez vendu à un prix réduit parce que je suis un de vos amis." "Ah oui, j'ai réduit le prix du charbon parce que vous êtes un de mes amis, mais parce que je suis un de vos amis j'ai réduit aussi la quantité de charbon que j'ai mis dans les sacs!"

LESSON TWENTY-SEVEN

HOW TO SAY "I BUILD"

The Infinitive of most verbs ends, as we know, in -er. In the previous lesson we saw that there are some which end in -re. There are also a few with an Infinitive in—ir. Such are *bâtir* (to build) and *finir* to (finish).

HERE is the Present Tense of *bâtir*:

je bâtis, I build	*nous bâtissons*
(tu bâtis)	*vous bâtissez*
il bâtit	*ils bâtissent*

All Present Participles end in -ant, and we can form the Imperfect Tense by dropping the -ant and adding -ais, -ait and so on.

Now, the Present Participle of *bâtir* is NOT *bâtant* but *bâtiss-ant*. So the Imperfect is:

je bâtissais, I was building	*nous bâtissions*
(tu bâtissais)	*vous bâtissiez*
il bâtissait	*ils bâtissaient*

The Past Participle is *bâti*: *j'ai bâti*, I (have) built.

How to Change, for Instance, the French for "Sad" into "Sadly"

We know that words such as "sad" or "happy" are adjectives. The words "sadly" and "happily" are known in English as adverbs. Such words usually have the effect of telling us how or in what way something is done. "He walks" simply describes an action. But "he walks slowly" (or "rapidly") tells us how or in what way the person walks. In English an adverb is usually formed by adding "-ly" to the adjective: "quick(ly)", "cheerful(ly)" and so on. In French adverbs are usually formed by adding -ment to the FEMININE of the adjective:

triste—triste (fem.), sad; *tristement,* sadly
heureux—heureuse (fem.), happy; *heureusement,* happily, fortunately
lent—lente (fem.), slow; *lentement,* slowly
rapide—rapide (fem.), quick, rapid; *rapidement,* quickly, rapidly

Not all adverbs in French are formed in quite this way, but this is the general rule. HERE is one exception to it:

bon, good   *bien,* well

Word List 27

finir, to finish   *choisir,* to choose
fini (Past Participle), finished   *choisi* (Past Participle), chosen
punir, to punish

Exercise 27 (*a*)

Put into English:

1. Les hommes qui bâtissaient une maison dans notre rue, ne travaillent pas aujourd'hui. 2. Si vous ne finissez pas votre travail, vous serez puni. 3. En regardant par ma fenêtre j'ai vu une vieille femme qui marchait très lentement. 4. De ces deux livres lequel choisissez-vous? 5. Hier Mme Dupont choisissait un cadeau pour sa petite fille. Elle est restée longtemps au magasin. 6. J'avais prêté ma bicyclette à mon voisin. Heureusement il me l'a rendue ce matin. 7. Les maisons qui sont bâties de briques sont meilleures que celles qui sont faites de bois. 8. Je finissais mon travail quand elle est entrée dans ma chambre. 9. Vous travaillez très lentement. Les autres ont fini déjà leur travail. 10. Le père de Jean ne le punissait jamais quand il était jeune; maintenant c'est un très méchant homme que les agents de police ont arrêté hier. 11. Quand nous étions jeunes nous choisissions toujours le chocolat au petit déjeuner; aujourd'hui nous préférons le café. 12. Je n'aime pas beaucoup cette maison que ces hommes bâtissent: elle est moins jolie que celle de notre voisin.

Exercise 27 (*b*)

Put into French:

1. I was choosing some postcards in a shop near the church. 2. I am sure that he will work well if you do not punish him. 3. Our neighbour has bought the house which they are building. 4. There are some people who walk very slowly. 5. I went up to his room on the fifth floor, but he was finishing his work. 6. Some bricks have fallen from the house which he was building. 7. Fortunately I have found the knife which I had lost. 8. The person who had taken it had not given it back to me. 9. Do not punish that young man. Why? He is a thief. 10. Those postcards which you were choosing are not very pretty. 11. I was looking for an ugly card. It is for my brother. 12. I have bought you some stamps. Which (ones) do you choose?

Have a Try 27

Les clients qui descendent à l'Hôtel Splendide sont, en général, très riches. Les personnes, qui n'ont pas beaucoup d'argent, choisissent des hôtels plus modestes.

M. Dupuy, qui était énormément riche, mais d'un caractère peu aimable, descendait toujours au Splendide quand il désirait passer deux ou trois jours à Paris.

Un matin au moment où il descendait de sa chambre il y a une panne (*break-down*) d'électricité. En conséquence l'ascenseur est resté immobile. M. Dupuy, très furieux, a fait de grands efforts pour ouvrir (*to open*) la porte de l'ascenseur, mais sans succès. Il est prisonnier.

A cet instant le petit fils d'une des femmes de chambre (*hotel maids*) montait l'escalier. Il avait été au marché où sa mère l'avait envoyé pour acheter des légumes. Ce petit garçon n'aimait pas M. Dupuy, qui était un homme détestable. Il n'a pas fait (*paid*) d'attention aux cris du prisonnier.

Il regarde un instant le captif et, choisissant une grande carotte, il la lui offre.

"Méchant animal," dit-il. "Je vous trouve dans une cage. Aimez-vous les carottes?"

LESSON TWENTY-EIGHT

HOW TO SAY "I SHALL BUILD" AND "I SHALL SELL"

We know (Lesson Twelve) that the Future of *donner* is formed by adding *-ai, -as, -a, -ons, -ez, -ont* to the Infinitive: *je donnerai* and so on. All Future tenses have these same endings. So with *bâtir* we do exactly the same. When the Infinitive of the verb ends in *-re* we drop the *e* before adding the endings. So we have:

je bâtirai, I shall build	*je vendrai*, I shall sell
(tu bâtiras)	*(tu vendras)*
il bâtira	*il vendra*
nous bâtirons	*nous vendrons*
vous bâtirez	*vous vendrez*
ils bâtiront	*ils vendront*

Now, as we know, the Conditional ("I should") of *donner* is formed by adding to it the endings *-ais, -ais, -ait, -ions, -iez, -aient*. All Conditionals have these same endings. So we can add them to the Infinitive *bâtir*, and to *vendre*, though here again we drop the final *e*.

je bâtirais, I should build	*je vendrais*, I should sell
(tu bâtirais)	*(tu vendrais)*
il bâtirait	*il vendrait*
nous bâtirions	*nous vendrions*
vous bâtiriez	*vous vendriez*
ils bâtiraient	*ils vendraient*

How to Say "Who?" and "Whom?"

We have already used *qui* with the meaning of "who", "which" and *que* with the meaning of "whom", "which", *qui* being the subject pronoun and *que* the object pronoun.

l'homme qui est à la porte, the man who is at the door
l'homme que j'ai vu, the man whom I saw
les vaches qui sont dans le champ, the cows which are in the field
les choses que vous achetez, the things which you buy.

114

qui and *que* as used in the above sentences are what are called relative pronouns. BUT we often use "who" and "which" to ask questions, that is as interrogative pronouns.

COMPARE these two:

The boy who is with you is the tallest in the school. *Le garçon qui est avec vous est le plus grand de l'école.*
Who is that tall boy? *Qui est ce grand garçon?*

The first *qui* is a relative pronoun, the second *qui* is an interrogative pronoun.

As subject of the verb *est* we use *qui* in both sentences.

Now compare these two:

the boy whom I saw, *le garçon que j'ai vu*
Whom did you see? *Qui avez-vous vu?*

So in RELATIVE sentences we use *qui* as subject and *que* as object. BUT in interrogative sentences *qui?* is used for both "who?" and "whom?". In both kinds of sentence *qui* is used after prepositions such as *à* and *de*.

le garçon de qui je parle, the boy of whom I am speaking
A qui (de qui) parlez-vous? To whom (of whom) are you speaking?

The relative *qui* and *que* can be used of people or of things.

l'homme qui est là, the man who was there
l'arbre qui est tombé, the tree which has fallen
la maison que je bâtis, the house which I build
le soldat que j'ai rencontré, the soldier whom I (have) met

BUT *qui?* interrogative means only "who?" or "whom?". It can be used only of people, not of things. So how are we to say "What have you done?" or "What has happened?"? "What?" as object of a verb is *que?* (or, before a vowel *qu'*). So "What have you done?" is *Qu-avez-vous fait?*

BUT with "what?" as subject of the verb we have to use *qu'est-ce qui?* (this is really "what is it which?").

What has happened? *Qu'est-ce qui est arrivé?*
Who has arrived? *Qui est arrivé?*
Whom have you seen? *Qui avez-vous vu?*
What are you looking for? *Que cherchez-vous?*

In fact, it is only "what?" as subject of a sentence, *qu'est-ce qui?* which is difficult.

Word List 28

entendre, to hear   *le bruit*, noise
attendre, to wait *or* to wait for

Exercise 28 (*a*)

Put into English:

1. Qui est ce monsieur qui a bâti cette maison? C'est un médecin. 2. Il m'a dit qu'il me vendrait son couteau, mais il l'a perdu. 3. Quel est ce bruit que j'ai entendu? Qu'avez-vous fait? 4. Je jetais des briques. Vous trouverez que la fenêtre de la salle à manger est cassée. 5. Qui est cette dame et que lui avez-vous dit? 6. Qui attendiez-vous quand je vous ai vu ce matin dans la place du marché? 7. Si elle n'est pas à la gare à six heures et demie, je ne l'attendrai pas. 8. Il y a une foule de personnes devant l'église: qu'est-ce qui arrive? 9. Je le punirais s'il était plus intelligent. Il travaille bien mais c'est le garçon le plus bête de la classe. 10. Qui cherchez-vous? Ma cousine. Elle m'a dit qu'elle serait ici à midi, mais elle n'est pas arrivée. 11. Que désirez-vous acheter? Des légumes et du fromage. 12. Qui vous a dit que le train de deux heures ne s'arrête pas ici? 13. Qu'est-ce qui arrivera s'il tombe dans cette eau profonde?

Exercise 28 (*b*)

Put into French:

1. Whom are you waiting for? 2. We are waiting for him. 3. What have you heard? 4. I heard the noise of the men who are cutting the trees. 5. What has he done? He has stolen some money. 6. Who are those people to whom you were speaking? 7. I am not sure when he will build his house. 8. I will sell you some wine. 9. If she does not walk quickly I shall not wait for her. 10. What will happen if the train has already departed? 11. What will you sell? 12. What did she say to you? 13. Who told you that the

train will not stop here? 14. There are always some free seats (places) in the trains which stop here. 15. Who is that young man whom the police have arrested? He is the farmer's son. 16. They made so much noise that the landlord heard them. 17. These vegetables are very good. Will you sell them to me? 18. Whom did you meet this morning? 19. Do you hear those birds? I do not hear them. 20. You would hear them, if there was less noise.

Have a Try 28

Mme Lebrun et les deux garçons attendaient l'arrivée de l'autobus dans lequel ils allaient monter pour retourner à Dieppe. Parmi la foule il y avait un homme qui, s'approchant avec précaution d'une dame, a pris le grand paquet qu'elle portait sous le bras (*arm*).

"C'est un voleur!" cria Jean. "Allons le chercher!" "Mais non," dit la dame qui, à la surprise de ses compagnons de voyage, n'a pas l'air d'être fâchée. "Mais nous aurions fait notre possible pour l'attraper, madame," dit Jean. "Merci," répond la dame, "mais ce sera le voleur qui ne sera pas content. Mon pauvre petit chat, qui était très vieux, est mort (*died*) hier. J'occupe un appartement en ville, mais j'ai une amie qui a un joli jardin. Elle a promis d'enterrer (*bury*) mon chat et c'est ce pauvre petit animal que le voleur trouvera dans le paquet qu'il a pris!"

LESSON TWENTY-NINE

MORE ABOUT NUMBERS

So far we know the numbers up to 61—*soixante et un*; 69 would therefore be *soixante-neuf*.

When we come to 70, however, we have to put *soixante-dix* (60-10), so that 71 is 60-11—*soixante et onze*.

When we come to 80 we reckon this as 4 times 20 and put *quatre-vingts*. There is no need to list every number, but the following list should be helpful:

60, *soixante*	90, *quatre-vingt-dix*
61, *soixante et un*	91, *quatre-vingt-onze*
62, *soixante-deux*	94, *quatre-vingt-quatorze*
69, *soixante-neuf*	99, *quatre-vingt-dix-neuf*
70, *soixante-dix*	100, *cent*
71, *soixante et onze*	101, *cent un*
72, *soixante-douze*	102, *cent deux*
78, *soixante-dix-huit*	200, *deux cents*
79, *soixante-dix-neuf*	201, *deux cent un*
80, *quatre-vingts*	1000, *mille* (in dates *mil*)
81, *quatre-vingt-un*	2000, *deux mille* (*deux milles* = 2 miles)
89, *quatre-vingt-neuf*	

TRY to REMEMBER that:

(1) There is an *et* in 21 up to 71 but not in 81, 91 or usually, in 101.

(2) That there is an *s* on *quatre-vingts* (80) and on 200, 300 and so on: *deux cents, trois cents*, but only when the number is exactly 80 or an exact 200 or 300: in other words no *s* on 81 or on 201.

(3) When there is no *et* there is a dash - in all numbers between 17 and 99.

In 153, for instance, we put *cent cinquante-trois*, putting the dash - only between that part of the number which comes between the limits of 17 and 99, in this case 53.

IN DATES we do not translate the English "and" unless, of course, there is already an *et* in the French number.

So 1964, *mil neuf cent soixante-quatre.* BUT 1921, *mil neuf cent vingt et un.*

WHEN talking about kings and queens we say "Henry the eighth". In French there is no *le* and save for "1st" (*premier*), the ordinary numbers *deux, trois* are used (as in dates of the month).

Charles the First (Charles I), *Charles premier*
Charles the Ninth (Charles IX), *Charles neuf*

The use of *en*

So FAR we have used *en* only as a preposition meaning "in": *en France*; *en silence.* In most cases we are more likely to use *dans*: *dans la ville.*

BUT *en* is also a pronoun and may mean "of it", "of them", "some", "from it", "from them". Like the object pronouns *me, le* and the rest, *en* comes in front of the verb.

IN ENGLISH, in answer to the question "Have you any money?" we may reply "Yes, I have" or "Yes, I have some" or (more likely) "No, I haven't (any)."

In French this "some" or "any" must be put in.

Avez-vous de l'argent? Oui, j'en ai or *J'en ai beaucoup* (I have a lot of it) or *Non, je n'en ai pas.*

IF there is another object pronoun *en* always comes second of the two. For instance, in reply to the question about money we might (rashly!) say:

Yes, I will lend you some. *Oui, je vous en prêterai.*

Word List 29

régner, to reign	*la collection*, collection
un accident, accident	*un an*, a year
la vitesse, speed (*also* gear)	

Exercise 29 (*a*)

Put into English:

1. Dans ce grand avion il y a des places pour cent vingt-cinq personnes. 2. Cet avion a volé de Paris à New York en huit heures et demie—une distance de trois mille milles ou

quatre mille huit cents kilomètres. 3. J'ai perdu votre
couteau : heureusement j'en ai un autre que je vous donnerai.
4. Le roi Louis quatorze a régné pendant soixante-douze ans.
5. Il a été roi de France de mil six cent quarante-trois jusqu'à
mil sept cent quinze. 6. Nous n'avons pas d'argent mais ma
sœur vous en prêtera. 7. Etes-vous sûr qu'elle nous atten-
dra ? Oui, j'en suis sûr, elle me l'a dit deux fois. 8. Cette
voiture qui a blessé un petit garçon pendant qu'il traversait
la rue allait trop vite. 9. Oui. Beaucoup trop vite. Elle
allait à une vitesse de cent cinq kilomètres à l'heure.
10. Combien de maisons y a-t-il dans la rue où vous demeu-
rez ? Il y en a quatre-vingt-douze. 11. Avez-vous beaucoup
de timbres-poste dans votre collection ? J'en ai quinze cents.
12. Mon oncle qui a beaucoup voyagé m'a envoyé des
timbres-poste. Je vous en donnerai une douzaine des meilleurs. 13. Merci beaucoup. Vous êtes très aimable. J'ai des
livres français que je vous prêterai, si vous n'en avez pas.
J'en ai deux ou trois qui sont très intéressants. 14. Qui est
cet auteur que nous avons rencontré au café ? C'est Monsieur Vite. Il a écrit cent trente-trois livres. Je lui ai dit
que j'en avais lu deux !

Exercise 29 (b)

Put into French:

1. An accident has happened to the train. Three travellers
have been killed and there are sixty-five (of them) who are
wounded. 2. Queen Victoria (has) reigned for (during)
sixty-four years. 3. She was the Queen of England from
1837 (in words) until 1901 (in words). 4. We haven't any
double rooms on the first floor, madam; but there are two
(of them) on the third floor. 5. They (refers to "rooms")
will be free this afternoon. Are you sure? Yes, I am sure.
6. I would not have bought these newspapers if I had known
that you have three already. 7. The motor-car into which
we had got (*monter*) was going at 85 kilometres per (to the)
hour. 8. Did you hear that noise during the night? Yes, I

was speaking of it to the landlord. 9. I have finished my letter, but I have no stamps. Have you any? 10. Yes. I bought a dozen (of them) at the café this morning. I will lend you two or three (of them). 11. Marseilles is at a distance of 800 kilometres from Paris. 12. I went to Paris for the first time in (*en* not *dans*) 1961 (in words).

Have a Try 29

News Items

1. Le Gouvernement examinera les circonstances de la catastrophe du train Calais–Paris qui a déraillé à l'entrée de la gare d'Abbeville. Cet accident a coûté la vie au mécanicien et à treize voyageurs et cent personnes ont été blessées.

2. A Los Angeles l'équipe d'Angleterre de football a battu celle des Etats Unis par 8 buts à 1. L'equipe du Real Madrid est partie pour Stuttgart où elle rencontrera celle de Reims (*Rheims*) en finale de la Coupe d'Europe de football.

3. Ce mois (*month*) marque une date de victoire pour la télévision. La première émission de télévision destinée simultanément à plusieurs (*several*) pays a eu lieu (*took place*) en 1954. Pendant sept jours dix-neuf programmes ont été retransmis et le Pape (*Pope*) a parlé dans leur langue nationale aux spectateurs de huit pays. L'Eurovision, qui avait transmis en 1953 le couronnement de la Reine d'Angleterre, a cessé (*ceased*) d'être un miracle.

(Adapted from *Le Figaro*)

LESSON THIRTY

HOW TO SAY "I HAVE HIDDEN MYSELF"

We saw in Lesson Twenty-five how to use verbs like *se cacher* when the subject and object of the verb refer to the same person (or thing).

We hide ourselves. *Nous nous cachons.*
He will hide himself. *Il se cachera.*

Now if we want to say "he has hidden himself" we should expect to use *il a*. In fact, however, with these "reflexive" verbs, as they are called, that is ones where the subject and object refer to the same person or thing, we use *il est*. This applies ONLY WHEN THE VERB IS USED REFLEXIVELY THUS:

He has hidden himself in the wood. *Il s'est caché dans les arbres.*

BUT

She has hidden him. *Elle l'a caché* (because the subject and object are two different people).

In Lesson Nineteen we learned the important rule that when a Past Participle has a tense of *avoir* (*a, avait* and so on) with it the participle agrees with its direct object, provided that this direct object comes BEFORE it. Now, with these reflexive verbs, although we are using *est* not *a*, the meaning is "has" not "is", and here, too, the Past Participle agrees with the direct object pronoun in front of it.

Tuer, to kill. So,

He has killed them. *Il les a tués.*

And

She (has) killed herself. *Elle s'est tuée.*

SIMILARLY with other tenses:

He would have killed her. *Il l'aurait tuée.*
She would have killed herself. *Elle se serait tuée.*

122

The Meaning of *on*

In English we sometimes use the word "one", not as a number, but in the more general sense of "people", "someone" or "they" not referring to anyone in particular. The French use *on* (third person singular) in the same way.

someone told me *or* I have been told, *on m'a dit*
French is spoken here (*notice in a shop window*). *Ici on parle français.*
One often finds rabbits in this field. *On trouve souvent des lapins dans ce champ.*

Word List 30

vrai, true	*quelquefois*, sometimes
un morceau, a bit, a piece	*un siècle*, century
la tête, head	

Exercise 30 (*a*)

Put into English:

1. La pauvre petite fille s'est tuée en tombant dans l'eau. 2. Si elle était tombée dans l'eau elle se serait tuée. 3. On m'a dit que vous alliez vendre votre maison. Est-ce vrai? 4. Je cherche mes deux frères. Les avez-vous vus? Où se sont-ils cachés? 5. Nous nous sommes habillés vite, parce que nous allions au bord de la mer. 6. On entend souvent des bruits dans ce bois pendant la nuit. 7. Pendant le seizième siècle on a bâti en France de très beaux châteaux. 8. Pourquoi êtes-vous entré dans ce petit magasin? Je cherchais de vieux livres. On en trouve quelquefois dans ces petits magasins. 9. Si vous vous étiez cachés dans le bois, on ne vous aurait pas trouvés. 10. Il est vrai qu'on a entendu quelqu'un qui entrait dans l'hôtel pendant la nuit. 11. On nous a dit qu'au quinzième siècle un général s'est tué dans une des chambres du palais. 12. Où est l'arbre dans lequel le roi Charles deux s'est caché? Il est tombé et on l'a coupé en morceaux.

Exercise 30 (*b*)

Put into French:

1. One often meets people (use *personne*) who have been to Paris. 2. Is it true that she has won the first prize? People have told me so (*le*). 3. The motor-car did not stop. The police have arrested the owner (of it). 4. We were looking for the boys, but they had hidden themselves. 5. Someone has shut the door and I haven't the key (of it). 6. The thieves wounded themselves in (*en*) entering the house by the window. 7. This bottle did not break itself! It is he who broke it. 8. The big book, which he had thrown out of (*par*)

the window, fell on the head of a policeman. 9. That poor old woman has thrown herself on the (railway) track in front of a train which was approaching. 10. Fortunately the train stopped, because it was going at a speed of 25 kilometres an (to the) hour. 11. During the eighteenth century, if you had taken a sheep or something which was not yours (to you) they (not *ils*) would have killed you. 12. She dressed herself very quickly, because she was going to meet her friends at half past seven.

Have a Try 30

"Vous rappelez-vous (*recall*, *remember*) la famille fran-çaise que nous avons rencontrée quand nous voyagions en

Normandie?" "Oui, très bien. Il y avait le père, la mère et
deux enfants." "Oui, c'est exact. Ils avaient pris déjà leurs
places quand nous sommes montés dans le train à Rouen et
j'ai pensé au commencement que j'allais les détester!"
"Moi, aussi. Le temps était beau mais la dame a insisté que
les fenêtres restent fermées." "Oui, mais c'était une dame
très aimable." "C'est vrai. Nous n'avions pas assez d'argent
pour aller déjeuner au wagon-restaurant." "Non, nous
avions acheté à la gare un petit paquet de chocolat."
"Oui. Et cette dame admirable, qui avait apporté du pain,
du jambon (*ham*) et des fruits pour le repas de la famille nous
a invités à en manger." "Et nous avons refusé—par polit-
esse! Heureusement elle a insisté!" "Oui, j'ai noté tous ces
détails dans mon journal (here 'diary', note-book) du
voyage."

LESSON THIRTY-ONE

HOW TO SAY "MINE" AND "OURS"

We know already how to use *mon*, *ma* and the rest. They are always used with nouns: *mon père*, *sa tante*.

In a sentence such as "this dog is mine" we don't want to have to say *ce chien est mon chien*, we want to know the French for "mine" to save repeating the word *chien*.

The following table will show us how to do this:

Masc. Sing.	Fem. Sing.	Masc. Pl.	Fem. Pl.	Eng.
le mien	la mienne	les miens	les miennes	mine
(le tien)	(la tienne)	(les tiens)	(les tiennes)	(thine)
le sien	la sienne	les siens	les siennes	his, hers
le nôtre	la nôtre	les nôtres	les nôtres	ours
le vôtre	la vôtre	les vôtres	les vôtres	yours
le leur	la leur	les leurs	les leurs	theirs

REMEMBER that *son* and *sa* can each mean either "his" or "her" because we have to go by the gender of the noun and not by the sex of the owner, so *son père* can be either "his father" or "her father", and *sa mère*, "her mother" or "his mother". In the same way *le sien* and *la sienne* can each mean either "his" or "hers". Which we put depends on the gender of the noun to which the possessive refers.

Our house is smaller than his (hers). *Notre maison est plus petite que la sienne.*

REMEMBER that although the plural of *notre* and *votre* is *nos*, *vos*, *le nôtre* and *le vôtre* merely add "s" to the singular *les nôtres*, *les vôtres*.

How to Say "I am right (wrong)"

There are some phrases where in English we use "to be" but the French use *avoir*.

For instance, "How old are you?" becomes in French "What age have you?"—*Quel âge avez-vous?* So the answer

is NOT *Je suis onze ans*, BUT, say, *J'ai onze ans* (I am eleven).
OTHER such expressions are:

to be right, *avoir raison*   to be sea-sick, *avoir le mal de mer*
to be wrong, *avoir tort*   to be in need of (to need), *avoir besoin de*

Word List 31

encore, still, yet   *le porte-monnaie*, purse

Exercise 31 (*a*)

Put into English:

1. Votre sœur n'est pas très grande. Quel âge a-t-elle?
Elle a quinze ans. 2. J'avais dix ans quand je suis allé pour
la première fois au bord de la mer. 3. Notre maison est
plus petite que la vôtre, mais nous préférons la nôtre parce
qu'elle a un très joli jardin. 4. Ma voiture est celle-ci: la
leur est devant l'hôtel. 5. Elle a perdu son porte-monnaie,
mais j'ai trouvé le mien. On l'avait mis sur cette table.
6. Vous avez raison: c'est lui qui a tort. 7. Si vous n'aviez
pas mangé tant de pommes vertes vous n'auriez pas le mal
de mer. 8. Vous aurez besoin de tout votre argent pour
acheter cette collection de timbres-poste. 9. Nous avons
trouvé notre chien, mais mon amie cherche le sien. 10. Où
est votre méchant petit neveu? Il n'est jamais là quand on a
besoin de lui. 11. Vos livres sont plus intéressants que les
nôtres, mais les siens sont encore meilleurs. 12. Votre tante
et la mienne ont quarante ans, mais mon oncle est plus
vieux que le vôtre.

Exercise 31 (*b*)

Put into French:

1. I am eight years old. (On) Thursday my father will be
thirty-nine years old. 2. How old was she when she came to
spend her holidays with you? She was seventeen years old.
3. Louis XIV was five years old when he became King of
France. 4. There are more sheep in our field than in hers.

5. There are more flowers in our room than in his. 6. You told me that he was fourteen years old, but you were wrong. 7. If you do not need those shoes, will you give them to me? 8. He told me that my brother and his had gone to the cinema. Was he right? 9. The room into which the gentleman went is not his: they gave him a room on the second floor. 10. How old is your dog? On Sunday he will be fourteen. And yours? Oh, he is still young. 11. I had lost my suitcase, but they have lent me theirs, which is bigger than mine. 12. I will give you my shoes. I shall not have need of them, because they have become too small.

Have a Try 31

L'heure du départ est arrivée. "Vous avez été bien aimable. Merci mille fois," dit Charles à Mme Lebrun et à Jean qui l'ont accompagné jusqu'au bureau de la Compagnie "Air France".

Une employée de la Compagnie s'approche d'un haut parleur et annonce, "Les passagers par Air France à destination de Londres sont priés de monter dans l'autobus."

A onze heures Charles et ses compagnons de voyage descendent de l'autobus à l'aéroport d'Orly. Le trajet (*trip*) dans le grand avion—c'est une "Caravelle" avec des places pour quatre-vingt quinze passagers—dure très peu de temps. En réponse aux questions d'un douanier (*customs officer*) Charles déclare qu'il n'y a pas de cigares dans sa valise, et qu'il n'a pas de montres cachées dans ses poches (*pockets*).

A la barrière il trouve sa mère qui est venue le rencontrer.

"Je suis sûre que vous vous êtes bien amusé en France," lui dit-elle. "Parlez-vous bien le français maintenant?"

"Mais non," répond Charles. "Mais j'ai fait de grands progrès."

(The author hopes that this may also be true of those who have worked through this book.)

"main"

PART II

KEY TO EXERCISES

Exercise 1 (a)

1. The boy is in the garden. 2. The actress is at the door of the house. 3. Where is the soldier? He is at the hotel. 4. Where is the woman? She is at the church. 5. The boys are in the street. 6. A cow and a sheep are in the garden behind the house. 7. The man who is at the hotel is an officer. 8. Where are the cows? They are in the field behind the church. 9. The actress who is in the street is the wife of the officer. 10. A soldier is at the door of the hotel with a woman who is the daughter of an actress.

Exercise 1 (b)

1. Le garçon est derrière un arbre dans le jardin. 2. L'officier est avec les soldats dans la rue. 3. Où sont les filles? Elles sont dans la maison. 4. Où sont les moutons? Ils sont dans le champ derrière l'hôtel. 5. Les filles de l'actrice sont dans l'église. 6. Le garçon est à la porte de l'hôtel. 7. La femme de l'officier est dans la rue. 8. Où sont les soldats? Ils sont dans le champ avec l'officier. 9. Une vache et un mouton sont dans le jardin. 10. La femme qui est à la porte de l'église est la fille de l'actrice. 11. L'homme et la femme sont dans les champs. 12. Où est la vache? Elle est dans le jardin.

Have a Try 1

The lion is a dangerous animal. In the Zoological Garden(s) in Paris and in London he (it) is in a cage. The spectator is behind a barrier. The hippopotamus—an

bottles of beer which he was going to send to the hotel.
5. I (have) told you that these shoes are mine: those belong
to the gentleman who is sitting at the table near the window.
6. I bought this book because it is more interesting than that
one. 7. There are ten people in that coach: let us get into
this one where we shall find some free (empty) seats. 8. We
have visited many castles, but we prefer this one because it is
more beautiful than all the others. 9. Which picture do you
prefer? This one or the one which I brought you? 10. We
were not sure in which train you would arrive—the two
o'clock (train) or the one which you took yesterday.
11. The green bicycle is not mine, but I will lend you this
one. 12. Where are your shoes? I have lost them: my cousin
has given me these.

Exercise 20 (b)

1. Qui était cette dame? Quelle dame? Celle qui regar-
dait les fleurs. 2. Dans quelle maison demeuriez-vous?
Dans celle-là. Elle a un joli jardin mais les chambres étaient
très petites. 3. De ces deux livres, nous préférons celui-ci,
parce que j'ai lu l'autre. 4. Montons dans cette voiture-ci:
il y a deux chiens et cinq enfants dans celle-là. 5. J'étais sûr
que je n'avais jamais vu cette vieille dame. Mais celle-ci qui
traverse la rue est une amie de ma tante. 6. Celle-ci est la
fenêtre qui est cassée: Regardez-la! 7. N'aviez-vous pas lu
dans le journal que la reine allait passer une semaine au
château? 8. Quel château? Celui que je vous ai montré
quand nous avons fait une excursion. 9. Il y a cinquante
personnes dans cet hôtel et toutes les tables sont occupées.
Non celle-ci est libre. 10. J'ai dit à ma sœur que je lui
avais écrit une longue lettre, mais elle ne l'a pas reçue.
11. Ces vaches-ci et celles-là sont à mon oncle. Nous avions
des vaches, mais nous les avons vendues. 12. Etes-vous le
méchant petit garçon qui a jeté cette brique-ci? Non,
madame, j'ai jeté celle-là!

Have a Try 20

Charles, who was tired, spent a good night. Jean and his mother are already in the hotel dining-room, and Charles arrives at the moment when the waiter brings the breakfast, which consists of a good cup of coffee or chocolate, with some bread and Norman(dy) butter. It is a less substantial meal than the English breakfast, but in France one has lunch an hour earlier than in England.

Exercise 21 (*a*)

1. I did not take your ten francs: it is that child there who found them. 2. If I had known that your friends were going to arrive by the ten o'clock train I would have met them at the station. 3. If you lend me two francs I shall have enough money (in order) to buy some fish and some fruit for lunch. 4. Who is that gentleman? He is John's uncle. It is he who bought our old car. 5. Who is that young man? That one? He is an American tourist. 6. What book are you buying? It is a book of the author whom we met at M. Leriche's (house). It is very interesting. 7. Look at those trees. We shall have some fine apples. 8. I should have had some beautiful fruit in my garden if your little nephew had not stolen it (them). 9. I do not like that gentleman. It is he who shut the door of the compartment at the moment when I wanted to get into the train. 10. Is it behind this tree that you put your bicycle? 11. I would have written to you if I had known in what hotel you were spending your holidays. 12. My aunt never travels by (in) plane: she thinks (that) it is dangerous.

Exercise 21 (*b*)

1. De ces deux tableaux c'est celui-ci que nous préférons. 2. Avez-vous assez d'argent pour acheter des légumes? 3. Avez-vous vu cette jeune dame. C'est la fille de notre

voisin. 4. Si j'avais su à quelle heure votre train arriverait je n'aurais pas marché si vite à la gare. 5. Ce n'est pas à cet hôtel-ci mais à celui-là que nous vous rencontrerons demain. 6. Est-ce lui ou sa sœur qui a gagné tous les prix? 7. C'est un homme extraordinaire! Il a un avion et deux grandes voitures, mais il voyage toujours à bicyclette. 8. Demain pour notre petit déjeuner nous aurons des tasses de café avec du pain et du beurre. 9. Ne montons pas dans ce compartiment-là. Dans celui-ci il y a quatre places qui sont libres. 10. Ne marchez pas si près de l'eau. C'est dangereux. 11. C'est un médecin excellent, mais nous ne l'aimons pas beaucoup. 12. Je ne travaillerai pas dans cette usine. J'aurais trop de travail.

Have a Try 21

While M. Lebrun is visiting a client, Jean and Charles are on a walk in the town. Mme Lebrun has lent her guide to her son and Charles has bought a plan of Rouen. They arrive without difficulty at the Place Notre Dame where the cathedral is situated. "Look at those two big towers," says Jean. "This one is the St. Romain Tower and that one is the Butter Tower." "Butter! Why? It's extraordinary." Jean consults his guide book. "Ah, yes. The gentleman who wrote this book gives us the explanation. In the good old times it was forbidden to Catholics to eat butter in Lent, but the bishop declared that the people who would give him money for the building of this tower would have his permission to eat butter in Lent." "That's very interesting," says Charles, "but if I was giving my money this tower would have received the name of the 'Chocolate Tower'!"

Exercise 22 (a)

1. I have told you twice that I shall be at the market at half-past two if the weather is fine. 2. Let us walk quickly, we have not much time. It is already twenty (minutes) to

three. 3. The performance will begin at eight o'clock (in the evening), but I will meet you in front of the theatre at a quarter-past seven. 4. Excuse me, sir, what time is it, please? 5. It is a quarter to nine, madam. Thank you (sir). 6. That young girl is very kind. I was going to get into that train, but she told me that our train will not be here before twenty-five past eleven. 7. It is five minutes to two by my watch. We shall have time to buy some newspapers and some postcards. 8. Walk more quickly, please. It will be already midnight when we (shall) arrive at our house (home). 9. In England we have lunch at one o'clock, but if you spend your holidays in France you will have lunch at noon. 10. If you get into this train you will be in Paris at a quarter-past six. 11. I should have met them if I had known at what time they would be at the station. 12. Is it noon already? No. It is half-past eleven.

Exercise 22 (b)

1. Il est trois heures et demie. J'ai pensé qu'elle serait ici avant deux heures. 2. Je l'ai vue deux fois, mais je ne lui ai jamais parlé. 3. A quelle heure serez-vous à la gare? A quatre heures moins quinze. 4. La représentation ne commencera pas avant huit heures et demie (du soir). 5. Si nous arrivons au théâtre à huit heures moins vingt, nous aurons le temps d'acheter des fruits et du chocolat. 6. Pardon, monsieur. Quelle heure est-il, s'il vous plaît? Il est dix heures vingt, madame. 7. Nous n'aurons pas assez de temps pour visiter le château. Il est déjà midi moins dix. 8. Nous ne serons pas chez nous avant minuit si nous ne marchons pas plus vite. 9. Quelle heure était-il quand vous l'avez vue hier? Il était six heures moins dix. 10. J'ai pensé que les magasins seraient fermés, parce qu'il était déjà cinq heures et demie. 11. Combien de fois avez-vous été à Paris? Trois ou quatre fois. C'est une belle ville. 12. Combien de temps avez-vous passé chez le médecin? Nous étions chez lui de trois heures jusqu'à quatre heures moins quinze.

Have a Try 22

At a quarter-past eleven Mme Lebrun and the two boys are at the seaside. After breakfast they walked to the station, where they took the express which brought them in a very short time to Dieppe. There they get into one of the buses which maintain the service (which run) between Dieppe and Le Tréport, and they get out of the bus at a nice little beach.

Jean and Charles look with satisfaction at the clear, calm sea. In five minutes they are in bathing-dresses.

Jean points to a rock which breaks the surface of the water at a distance of thirty metres. "I bet that I shall arrive at that rock before you," he says.

The two boys begin to swim with all their strength (might). The (his) head plunged in the water, Charles does not notice an old gentleman in front of him and collides violently with him. When he has apologised to him Jean is already sitting on the rock.

Exercise 23 (a)

1. No, sir, Mme Dupont is not at home. She set out this morning for the country. 2. If those little boys had not got into that wretched little boat they would not have fallen into the water. 3. Yesterday we went to Paris for the first time. 4. Our hotel is very large. We have a nice room on the fourth floor. 5. She was going to spend her holidays at the seaside, but she came back to Paris after five days. 6. At school she used always to be (the) first in her class, but she has become very lazy. 7. We made a nice excursion, but my aunt, who was ill, remained in the hotel. 8. The landlord went down to the cellar to look for a bottle of white wine. 9. If you had walked more quickly we should have arrived home at lunch-time. 10. When I arrived at M. Dubois' house, his sister told me that he had already set out for Bordeaux. 11. It is the tenth day of our holidays. It is also

the ninth day of bad weather   12. She did not tell us that
she had come back by air (by aeroplane).

Exercise 23 (b)

1. A quelle heure est-elle arrivée chez vous? A minuit.
2. J'étais monté à ma chambre au septième étage. 3. Il est allé
à Paris mais se sœur est restée chez elle. 4. Nous sommes allés
(entrés) dans l'hôtel mais nos amis étaient partis déjà pour
le bord de la mer. 5. Nous demeurons dans la première
maison de la rue. Elle a une porte verte. 6. J'ai acheté
trois billets pour la deuxième représentation de ce soir.
Elle commence à huit heures et demie. 7. Nous ne serions
pas revenus si nous avions su que vous n'étiez pas chez vous.
8. Quand nous sommes arrivés à la gare le train était parti
déjà. 9. Les agents de police sont descendus à la cave où ils
ont trouvé deux jeunes voleurs qui étaient cachés derrière les
bouteilles. 10. Mme Dupont est très fâchée. Elle est montée
jusqu'au neuvième étage et en arrivant à sa porte elle a
trouvé qu'elle avait perdu sa clef. 11. Quand je l'ai vue pour
la première fois elle était jeune. Maintenant elle est devenue
très vieille. 12. Quand sont-ils revenus du bord de la mer?
Ils sont arrivés chez eux hier à sept heures et demie.

Have a Try 23

In Paris there are many houses which have no lift. For
this reason a person who occupies a flat on the first floor is in
general under the necessity of paying a higher rent than the
tenant of a flat on the sixth floor.

M. Billot was not rich, and that is why the flat where he
was passing his old age was on the seventh floor. The old
gentleman had in his room a grandfather clock. One day he
noticed with regret that the clock, which he liked very much,
was not going well. A clock-maker came to take the clock
away to repair it.

Five days later a man got out of a delivery van in front of

the house and began to climb the stairs, carrying the clock, which was now in good condition. At this moment a young man, who also lived in the house, saw the porter, who was coming up with difficulty because the big clock was very heavy.

"My friend," he said to him innocently, "if you want to know the time, why don't you wear (carry) a watch? It would be much simpler!"

Exercise 24 (*a*)

1. Which of these two bicycles belongs to you? This one belongs to me. 2. The gentleman to whom I sold my car has departed for the country. 3. To which of these gentlemen did you lend my newspaper? To that one. 4. The knife with which you have cut the bread is better than this one. 5. The rooms on the fifth floor are smaller than those on (of) the first, but they are less dear. 6. Of all the hotels in (of) this town the "Station Hotel" is the biggest, but at the "Black Horse" the meals are better. 7. Mme Chose is younger than my aunt, but she is much less pleasant. 8. There are fifty-five rooms in this hotel. Which is the one of your friends? 9. This author has written many books. Which do you prefer? 10. The landlord has given me two keys. Which is the one of your room? 11. I saw a thief who was getting through a window into one of these houses. But which? 12. Our neighbour is richer than we are; he travels first class, and in hotels he always has the best bedroom.

Exercise 24 (*b*)

1. Nous avons deux chambres qui sont libres. Laquelle préférez vous? 2. Dans laquelle de ces deux chambres avez-vous mis ma valise? Dans celle-là, madame. 3. A laquelle de ces filles avez-vous donné ma clef? 4. Auquel de ces deux garçons avez-vous prêté mon couteau? 5. Le château que nous avons visité hier est plus grand que celui-ci. 6. Si vous

allez à l'Hôtel de la Gare vous aurez une jolie chambre, mais ici les repas sont beaucoup meilleurs. 7. Nous avons vendu la maison dans laquelle nous demeurions. 8. Il y a beaucoup de cafés dans cette ville. Dans lequel est-il entré? 9. Le cheval est plus intelligent que le mouton, mais l'éléphant est le plus intelligent de tous les animaux. 10. De quel homme parliez-vous? Du médecin. 11. Duquel de ces deux messieurs parliez-vous? De celui-là. 12. La ville à laquelle il est allé est près de la mer.

Have a Try 24

"Where are you going to spend your holidays, my friend?" "In Paris. It will be my first visit." "In that case I advise you to lodge (put up) at a hotel near the Place St. Michel." "Why?" "Because in that part of the town there are hotels where you will find all the comfort which you want at a reasonable price." "Yes. But I should be (at) a considerable distance from the centre of Paris, and if I am forced to get into a taxi to go to the Cathedral, to the Louvre or to the big shops, I shall not have enough money to pay for my room at the hotel or (for) my meals in a restaurant." "(But) no, there is an excellent bus-service and you also have the Underground."

Exercise 25 (a)

1. The train is stopping because an old cow is sitting on the track: there are some travellers who are very annoyed! 2. On Monday the first of January we went to the theatre. 3. On Thursday the 28th of July we departed by air for France. 4. Don't cross the track at the moment when (where) a train is approaching. 5. The hunter has not killed the tiger. He has wounded it and the poor animal is hiding in the grass. 6. On the 5th of November the police(men) arrested many people who were throwing squibs in the street. 7. If you fall into this deep water you will kill your-

self. 8. From the 20th of August until the 6th of September I shall be at the seaside with my father. 9. When did you come back from Paris? We arrived home on Saturday, the 30th of July. 10. If you don't dress quickly you will have no breakfast. 11. If we hide in the cellar they will not find us. 12. If you are not careful you will wound yourself. Those big knives are dangerous.

Exercise 25 (b)

1. Si le train ne s'arrête pas à cette petite gare nous marcherons jusqu'à la ville. 2. Jeudi nous n'allons pas à l'école et nos vacances commenceront le quinze décembre. 3. Si vous jetez ces pétards vous blesserez quelqu'un. 4. Vous vous tuerez si vous n'êtes pas prudent. 5. Un mouton a été tué parce qu'il traversait la voie pendant que le train s'approchait. 6. Je suis sûr que ces garçons ne sont pas allés à l'école. Où se cachent-ils? 7. Le chien a caché le poisson dans le lit de ma tante. Elle sera très fâchée! 8. Vendredi le treize juin nous serons à Paris. 9. Nous nous habillons très vite quand nous sommes au bord de la mer. 10. Ma sœur est partie pour Londres le premier avril et elle est revenue ici le deux mai. 11. Pardon, madame. Les trains ne s'arrêtent pas ici. Cette gare est fermée. 12. Elle se blessera si elle n'est pas prudente.

Have a Try 25

"You told me that in Paris it is possible to go without difficulty by bus from the Place St. Michel, for instance, to the Place de l'Opéra." "Yes, it is very simple and, if you buy a booklet of tickets, you will find that it will be less dear than to buy a ticket each time that you get into a bus. If you go by (the) Underground it is possible to change train(s) once or twice and your ticket remains valid until you go up to the surface.

"At the entrance of a Métro station there is always a plan

which marks all the lines, and I am certain that you will have
no difficulty in finding if it is necessary or not to change in
order to arrive at your destination."

Exercise 26 (*a*)

1. While I was going down the stairs I met an American
tourist who was going up to the fourth floor. 2. This old
woman used to sell fruit and vegetables in (at) the market.
3. This old gentleman is very poor: if you do not want to
buy my old bicycle I will give it to him. 4. My friend will not
lend you his car because he has sold it to me. 5. This gentleman is very angry because he lent me his suitcase yesterday
and I have not given it back to him. 6. If you do not give
me back the money which you have stolen the policeman will
arrest you. 7. I wrote a long letter to my cousin, but I did
not send it to her. 8. Why? Because I hadn't any stamps.
9. I will lend you a franc to buy some stamps if you give it
me back this afternoon. 10. If you go down into the cellar
you will find some bottles of red wine which is very good.
11. Who gave them to you? It is my brother who gave them
to me. He received them from a friend. 12. If I had not
sold my car I would have lent it to you.

Exercise 26 (*b*)

1. Je lui donne de l'argent. 2. Il me vend des timbres-
poste. 3. Je les lui donne. 4. Il me les vend. 5. Je vous le
donnerai. 6. Nous la lui donnerons. 7. Je vous les mon-
trerai. 8. Nous la leur vendions. 9. Il nous l'a prêté. 10. Il
vous l'a prêtée. 11. Je ne le lui ai pas envoyé. 12. Je ne la
leur ai pas envoyée.

Exercise 26 (*c*)

1. Si vous descendez à la salle à manger vous trouverez
des tasses sur la table. 2. Je lui ai prêté de l'argent, mais il ne

me l'a pas rendu. 3. Pourquoi ne vous l'a-t-il pas rendu?
4. Quelqu'un m'a vendu de très bons timbres-poste. 5. J'ai
une vieille bicyclette. Je vous la prêterai. 6. Je ne la lui
prêterai pas. 7. Pourquoi ne nous la prêterez-vous pas?
8. Si j'avais su que vous aviez lu ce livre je ne vous l'aurais
pas envoyé. 9. Ils nous l'auraient envoyé. 10. Ne vous les
a-t-il pas rendus?

Have a Try 26

One day a Norman farmer went to visit his neighbour who
was (a) coal merchant. "I have come to ask you a little
service (favour)," he says to him. "What service?" "It is a
question of the coal which I want to buy." "Yes. In those
sacks there is some coal which is very good. If, for instance,
you want ten sacks I sell them to you at ten francs the sack."
"That's dear enough," answers the farmer. "The little
service of which I spoke is that you sell me this coal at a
reduced price, because I am one of your best friends." "You
are asking me (for) something exceptional," answers the
merchant, "but since you are my friend I sell you this coal
at eight francs."

The farmer went away very pleased, but a month after he
came back. "This coal burns very quickly," he says. "I am
speaking of the coal which you sold to me at a reduced price
because I am one of your friends." "Ah, yes. I reduced the
price of the coal because you are one of my friends, but
because I am one of your friends I also reduced the quantity
of coal which I put in the sacks!"

Exercise 27 (a)

1. The men who were building a house in our street are
not working today. 2. If you do not finish your work you
will be punished. 3. On looking out of my window I saw an
old woman who was walking very slowly. 4. Of these two
books which do you choose? 5. Yesterday Mme Dupont

was choosing a present for her little daughter. She remained
for a long time in the shop. 6. I had lent my bicycle to my
neighbour. Fortunately he (has) returned it to me this
morning. 7. Houses which are built of brick are better than
those which are made of wood. 8. I was finishing my work
when she came into my room. 9. You work very slowly.
The others have already finished their work. 10. John's
father never punished him when he was young. Now he is a
very bad man whom the police arrested yesterday. 11. When
we were young we always chose chocolate at breakfast;
today we prefer coffee. 12. I don't much like this house
which these men are building; it is less pretty than our
neighbour's.

Exercise 27 (b)

1. Je choisissais des cartes postales dans un magasin près
de l'église. 2. Je suis sûr qu'il travaillera bien si vous ne le
punissez pas. 3. Notre voisin a acheté la maison qu'ils
bâtissent. 4. Il y a des personnes qui marchent très lentement. 5. Je suis monté à sa chambre au cinquième étage
mais il finissait son travail. 6. Des briques sont tombées de
la maison qu'il bâtissait. 7. Heureusement j'ai trouvé le
couteau que j'avais perdu. 8. La personne qui l'avait pris
ne me l'avait pas rendu. 9. Ne punissez pas ce jeune homme.
Pourquoi? C'est un voleur. 10. Ces cartes postales que
vous choisissiez ne sont pas très jolies. 11. Je cherchais
une vilaine carte postale. C'est pour mon frère. 12. Je vous
ai acheté des timbres-poste. Lesquels choisissez vous?

Have a Try 27

The clients who put up at the "Hotel Splendide" are, in
general, very rich. People who have not much money
choose more modest hotels.

M. Dupuy, who was enormously rich, but of a far from

amiable disposition, always stayed at the Splendide when he wanted to spend two or three days in Paris.

One morning at the moment when (where) he was coming down from his room there was an electrical breakdown. In consequence, the lift remained motionless. M. Dupuy, very angry, made great efforts to open the door of the lift, but without success. He is (a) prisoner. At this instant the small son of one of the hotel maids was coming up the stairs. He had been to the market, where his mother had sent him to buy vegetables. This little boy did not like M. Dupuy, who was a hateful man. He paid no attention to the cries of the prisoner. For an instant he looks at the captive and, choosing a large carrot, he offers it to him. "Tiresome animal!" he says. "I find you in a cage. Do you like carrots?"

Exercise 28 (a)

1. Who is this gentleman who has built this house? He is a doctor. 2. He told me that he would sell me his knife, but he has lost it. 3. What is that noise that I heard? What have you done? 4. I was throwing bricks. You will find that the dining-room window is broken. 5. Who is that lady, and what did you say to her? 6. Whom were you waiting for when I saw you this morning in the market-place? 7. If she is not at the station at half-past six, I will not wait for her. 8. There are a crowd of people in front of the church. What is happening? 9. I would punish him if he were more intelligent. He works well but he is the stupidest boy in (of) the class. 10. Whom are you looking for? My cousin. She told me that she would be here at midday (noon), but she hasn't arrived. 11. What do you want to buy? Some vegetables and some cheese. 12. Who told you that the two o'clock train does not stop here? 13. What will happen if he falls into this deep water?

Exercise 28 (b)

1. Qui attendez-vous? 2. Nous l'attendons. 3. Qu'avez-vous entendu? 4. J'ai entendu le bruit des hommes qui coupent les arbres. 5. Qu'a-t-il fait? Il a volé de l'argent. 6. Qui sont ces personnes à qui vous parliez? 7. Je ne suis pas sûr quand il bâtira sa maison. 8. Je vous vendrai du vin? 9. Si elle ne marche pas vite je ne l'attendrai pas. 10. Qu'est-ce qui arrivera si le train est parti déjà? 11. Que vendrez-vous? 12. Que vous a-t-elle dit? 13. Qui vous a dit que le train ne s'arrêtera pas ici? 14. Il y a toujours des places libres dans les trains qui s'arrêtent ici. 15. Qui est ce jeune homme que les agents de police ont arrêté? C'est le fils du fermier. 16. Ils ont fait tant de bruit que le propriétaire les a entendus. 17. Ces légumes sont très bons. Me les vendrez-vous? 18. Qui avez-vous rencontré ce matin? 19. Entendez-vous ces oiseaux-là? Je ne les entends pas. 20. Vous les entendriez, s'il y avait moins de bruit.

Have a Try 28

Mme Lebrun and the two boys were waiting for the arrival of the bus into which they were going to get in order to return to Dieppe. Among the crowd there was a man who, approaching a lady cautiously, took the large parcel which she was carrying under her arm.

"He's a thief!" cried Jean. "Let us go and look for him." "(But), no," said the lady, who, to the surprise of her travelling companions, has not the appearance (does not look) of being annoyed. "But we would have done our utmost to catch him, madam," says Jean. "Thank you," answered the lady, "but it will be the thief who will not be pleased. My poor little cat, who was very old, died yesterday. I occupy a flat in town, but I have a friend who has a nice garden. She promised to bury my cat, and it is this poor little animal which the thief will find in the parcel which he has taken."

Exercise 29 (a)

1. In this big plane there are places for one hundred and twenty-five people. 2. This plane has flown from Paris to New York in eight and a half hours—a distance of three thousand miles or four thousand eight hundred kilometres. 3. I have lost your knife. Fortunately I have another which I will give you. 4. The king Louis XIV reigned for seventy two years. 5. He was King of France from 1643 until 1715. 6. We haven't any money, but my sister will lend you some. 7. Are you sure that she will wait for us? Yes. I am sure of it. She told me so twice. 8. That car which wounded a small boy while he was crossing the street was going too fast. 9. Yes. Much too fast. It was going at a speed of one hundred and five kilometres an hour. 10. How many houses are there in the street in which you live? There are ninety two. 11. Have you many stamps in your collection? I have fifteen hundred. 12. My uncle who has travelled much has sent me some stamps. I will give you a dozen of the best of them. 13. Thank you very much. You are very kind. I have some French books which I will lend you, if you haven't any. I have two or three which are very interesting. 14. Who is that author whom we met at the café? He is M. Vite. He has written one hundred and thirty-three books. I told him that I had read two of them.

Exercise 29 (b)

1. Un accident est arrivé au train. Trois voyageurs ont été tués et il y en a soixante-cinq qui sont blessés. 2. La Reine Victoria a régné pendant soixante-quatre ans. 3. Elle était (a été) la Reine d'Angleterre de mil huit cent trente-sept jusqu'à mil neuf cent un. 4. Nous n'avons pas de chambres à deux lits au premier étage, madame, mais il y en a deux au troisième (étage). 5. Elles seront libres cet après-midi. En êtes-vous sûr? Oui, j'en suis sûr. 6. Je n'aurais pas acheté ces journaux si j'avais su que vous en

avez déjà trois. 7. La voiture dans laquelle nous étions
montés allait à quatre-vingt-cinq kilomètres à l'heure.
8. Avez-vous entendu ce bruit pendant la nuit? Oui, j'en
parlais au propriétaire. 9. J'ai fini ma lettre mais je n'ai
pas de timbres-poste. En avez-vous? 10. Oui. J'en ai
acheté une douzaine ce matin au café. Je vous en prêterai
deux ou trois. 11. Marseille(s) est à une distance de huit
cents kilomètres de Paris. 12. Je suis allé à Paris pour la
première fois en mil neuf cent soixante et un.

Have a Try 29

1. The Government will examine the circumstances of the
catastrophe to (of) the Calais to Paris train which came off
the rails at the entrance to Abbeville station. This accident
cost the life of the driver and of (to) thirteen travellers, and
a hundred people were wounded (injured).

2. At Los Angeles the English (England) football team
beat that of the United States by 8 goals to 1.

The team of Real Madrid has set out for Stuttgart, where
it will meet the Rheims side in the final of the European
Football Cup.

3. This month marks a victorious date for television. The
first broadcast of television, intended simultaneously for
several countries, took place in 1954. During seven days
nineteen programmes were retransmitted and the Pope spoke
in their native language to the viewers of eight countries.
Eurovision which had transmitted the coronation of the
Queen of England in 1953 has ceased to be a miracle.

Exercise 30 (a)

1. The poor little girl has killed herself in falling into the
water. 2. If she had fallen into the water she would have
killed herself. 3. Someone has told me that you were going
to sell your house. Is it true? 4. I am looking for my two

brothers. Have you seen them? Where have they hidden themselves? 5. We dressed (ourselves) quickly because we were going to the seaside. 6. One often hears noises in this wood during the night. 7. During the sixteenth century they built some very fine castles in France. 8. Why did you go into this little shop? I was looking for some old books. One (you) find(s) some sometimes in these little shops. 9. If you had hidden yourselves in the wood they would not have found you. 10. It is true that people heard someone who was entering the hotel during the night. 11. We have been told (people have told us) that in the fifteenth century a general killed himself in one of the rooms in the palace. 12. Where is the tree in which King Charles II hid himself? It fell and they have cut it in pieces.

Exercise 30 (b)

1. On rencontre souvent des personnes qui ont été à Paris. 2. Est-il vrai qu'elle a gagné le premier prix? On me l'a dit. 3. La voiture ne s'est pas arrêtée. Les agents en ont arrêté le propriétaire. 4. Nous cherchions les garçons mais ils s'étaient cachés. 5. On a fermé la porte et je n'en ai pas la clef. 6. Les voleurs se sont blessés en entrant dans la maison par la fenêtre. 7. Cette bouteille ne s'est pas cassée! C'est lui qui l'a cassée. 8. Le grand livre qu'il avait jeté par la fenêtre est tombé sur la tête d'un agent de police. 9. Cette pauvre vieille femme s'est jetée sur la voie devant un train qui s'approchait. 10. Heureusement le train s'est arrêté, parce qu'il allait à une vitesse de vingt-cinq kilomètres à l'heure. 11. Pendant le dix-huitième siècle, si vous aviez pris un mouton ou quelquechose qui n'était pas à vous, on vous aurait tué. 12. Elle s'est habillée très vite, parce qu'elle allait rencontrer ses amis à sept heures et demie.

Have a Try 30

"Do you remember the French family whom we met when we were travelling in Normandy?" "Yes, very well. There were the father, the mother and two children." "Yes, that's right. They had already taken their places when we got into the train at Rouen, and I thought at the beginning that I was going to hate them." "I also (so did I). The weather was fine but the mother insisted that the windows remain shut." "Yes, but she was a very nice lady." "That's true. We hadn't enough money to go and lunch in the restaurant car." "No. We had bought in the station a small packet of chocolate." "Yes. And this admirable woman, who had brought bread, ham and fruit for the family's lunch invited us to eat some." "And we refused— out of politeness!" "Fortunately she insisted!" "Yes. I noted (down) all these details in my diary of the journey."

Exercise 31 (a)

1. Your sister is not very big. How old is she? She is fifteen. 2. I was ten years old when I went to the seaside for the first time. 3. Our house is smaller than yours, but we prefer ours because it has a very nice garden. 4. My car is this one; theirs is in front of the hotel. 5. She has lost her purse but I have found mine. Someone had put it on this table. 6. You are right; it is he who is wrong. 7. If you hadn't eaten so many green apples, you would not be seasick. 8. You will need all your money (in order) to buy this collection of postage stamps. 9. We have found our dog, but my friend is looking for hers. 10. Where is your naughty little nephew? He is never there when one needs him. 11. Your books are more interesting than ours but his (hers) are still better. 12. Your aunt and mine are forty years old, but my uncle is older than yours.

Exercise 31 (*b*)

1. J'ai huit ans. Jeudi mon père aura trente-neuf ans.
2. Quel âge avait-elle quand elle est venue passer ses vacances avec vous? Elle avait dix-sept ans. 3. Louis quatorze
avait cinq ans quand il est devenu roi de France. 4. Il y a
plus de moutons dans notre champ que dans le sien. 5. Il y
a plus de fleurs dans notre chambre que dans la sienne.
6. Vous m'avez dit qu'il avait quatorze ans, mais vous aviez
tort. 7. Si vous n'avez pas besoin de ces souliers, me les
donnerez-vous? 8. Il m'a dit que mon frère et le sien étaient
allés au cinéma. Avait-il raison? 9. La chambre dans
laquelle le monsieur est entré n'est pas la sienne; on lui a
donné une chambre au deuxième étage. 10. Quel âge a
votre chien? Dimanche il aura quatorze ans. Et le vôtre?
Oh, il est encore jeune. 11. J'avais perdu ma valise, mais ils
m'ont prêté la leur qui est plus grande que la mienne.
12. Je vous donnerai mes souliers. Je n'en aurai pas besoin
parce qu'ils sont devenus trop petits.

Have a Try 31

The time for (hour of) departure has come. "You have
been very kind. Thank you a thousand times," says Charles
to Mme Lebrun and Jean, who have accompanied him as far
as the "Air France" office. An employee of the Company
approaches a loud-speaker and announces: "The passengers
by Air France bound for London are requested to get into
the bus."

At eleven o'clock Charles and his travelling companions
get out of the bus at Orly airport. The trip in the big plane—
it is a "Caravelle" with seats for ninety-five passengers—
lasts very little time. In reply to the question of a Customs
Officer Charles declares that there are no cigars in his suitcase, and that he has no watches hidden in his pockets.

At the barrier he finds his mother, who has come to meet
him.

"I am sure that you enjoyed yourself in France," she says to him. "Do you speak French well now?"

"(But) no," answers Charles. "But I have made great progress."

ALPHABETICAL WORD LIST

(Numerals, Days of the Week and Months are not included in this general vocabulary, since they are given in separate lists in the lessons concerned with them.)

A

à, to, at, in
acheter, to buy
accident (m.), accident
actrice (f.), actress
agent de police (m.), policeman
aimable, kind, nice
aimer, to like, love
aller, to go
américain, American
ami(e) (m.)(f.), friend
an (m.), year
anglais, English
Angleterre (f.), England
animal (m.), animal
après, after, afterwards
après-midi (m. or f.), afternoon
apporter, to bring
s'approcher (*de*), approach, to draw near (to)
arbre (m.), tree
argent (m.), money, silver
arrêter, to stop, to arrest
s'arrêter, to stop (oneself), come to a halt
arriver, to arrive
assez, enough, sufficient
assis, seated, sitting
attendre, to wait, to wait for
attraper, to catch
aujourd'hui, today
aussi, also
auteur (m.), author
autobus (m.), motorbus
autre, other
avant, before (of time)
avec, with
avion (m.), aeroplane
avoir, to have

B

bateau (m.), boat
bâtir, to build
beau, beautiful, fine
beaucoup, much, many
bête, stupid, (f.) beast
beurre (m.), butter
bicyclette (f.), bicycle
bien, well
bientôt, soon
bière (f.), beer
billet (m.), ticket
blanc(he), white
blesser, to wound
bois (m.), wood
bon, good
bord (m.), edge
bord de la mer, seaside
bottine (f.), boot
boulanger (m.), baker
bouteille (f.), bottle
brique (f.), brick
bruit (m.), noise
bu, drunk

C

cacher, to hide
cadeau (m.), present
café (m.), coffee, café
cage (f.), cage
cahier (m.), exercise-book, note-book
campagne (f.), country (as opposed to town)
carte (f.), map
carte-postale (f.), postcard
casser, to break
cave (f.), cellar
ce, this, that

celui, this (one), that (one)
cent, a hundred
certain, certain
chaise (f.), chair
chambre (f.), room, bedroom
champ (m.), field
chapeau (m.), hat
chasseur (m.), hunter
cher, dear
chercher, to seek, look for
cheval (m.), horse
cheveu (m.), hair
chez, to, at the house (home) of
chien (m.), dog
chocolat (m.), chocolate
choisir, to choose
chose (f.), thing
cinéma (m.), cinema
classe (f.), class, class-room
clef (f.), key
collection (f.), collection
combien?, how much (many)?
commencer, to begin
compartiment (m.), compartment
couper, to cut
courageux, courageous, brave
cousin(e) (m., f.), cousin
couteau (m.), knife
crayon (m.), pencil

D

dame (f.), lady
dans, in, into
de, from, of
déjà, already
déjeuner (m.), lunch
petit déjeuner, breakfast
demain, tomorrow
demeurer, to live, dwell
demi(e), half
derrière, behind
descendre, to go down, come down, put up at
désirer, to wish (to), want (to)
devant, before (of place), in front of

devenu, become
difficile, difficult
dîner (m.), dinner
dîner, to dine, have dinner
distance (f.), distance
dit, said, told
donner, to give
douzaine (f.), dozen
dur, hard

E

eau (f.), water
école (f.), school
écrit, written
église (f.), church
éléphant (m.), elephant
elle, she, her,
en, in, of it, some
enfant (m., f.), child
énorme, enormous
entendre, to hear
entre, between
entrer, to enter, go in
envoyer, to send
escalier (m.), stairs, staircase
et, and
étage (m.), floor
été, been
être, to be
eu, had
excursion (f.), excursion, outing
extraordinaire, extraordinary

F

fâché, cross, angry
fait, done, made
femme (f.), woman, wife
fenêtre (f.), window
fermer, to shut
fermier (m.), farmer
fermière (f.), farmer's wife
fille (f.), girl, daughter
fils (m.), son
finir, to finish
fleur (f.), flower
fleuve (m.), river

fois (f.), time(s)
franc (m.), franc
français, French
France (f.), France
frère (m.), brother
fromage (m.), cheese
fruit (m.), fruit

G

gagner, to earn, win, gain
garçon (m.), boy, waiter
gare (f.), (railway) station
gâteau (m.), cake
grand, big, great, tall
gris, grey

H

(s')habiller, to dress (oneself)
haut, high
heure (f.), hour, o'clock, time (of day)
histoire (f.), story, history
homme (m.), man
horloge (f.), clock
hôtel (m.), hotel

I

ici, here
intelligent, intelligent, clever
intéressant, interesting
italien, Italian
inviter (à), to invite (to)

J

jardin (m.), garden
Jean, John
jeter, to throw
jeune, young
joli, pretty, nice
jour (m.), day
journal (m.), newspaper
jusqu'à, until, as far as, up to

K

kilogramme (m.), kilogram(me)
kilomètre (m.), kilometre

L

là, there
lait (m.), milk
le (la), the
légume (m.), vegetable
lent(ement), slow(ly)
lequel, which (one)
lettre (f.), letter
libre, free, vacant
lit (m.), bed
livre (m.), book
Londres, London
long(ue), long
longtemps, (for) a long time
lu, read

M

madame, Madam, Mrs.
mademoiselle, miss
magasin (m.), shop
main (f.), hand
maintenant, now
mais, but
maison (f.), house
malade, ill
malheureux, unhappy
manger, to eat
marchand (m.), merchant, shop-keeper
marché (m.), market
marcher, to walk, to march
marée (f.), tide
matin (m.), morning
méchant, wicked, naughty, wretched
médecin (m.), doctor
meilleur, better
mer (f.), sea
merci, thank you
mère (f.), mother
midi (m.), midday
mille, thousand, a mile
mil, thousand (in dates)
minuit (m.), midnight
minute (f.), minute

mis, put
moins, less
moment (m.), moment
mon (*ma*), my
monde (m.), world
monter, to go up, get into
montre (f.), watch
montrer, to show
morceau (m.), piece, bit
mouton (m.), sheep, mutton

N

ne . . . jamais, never
ne . . . pas, not
neveu (m.), nephew
nez (m.), nose
nièce (f.), niece
noir, black
non, no
nuit (f.), night

O

occupé, occupied, taken
œuf (m.), egg
officier (m.), officer
oiseau (m.), bird
oncle (m.), uncle
ou, or
où, where
oui, yes

P

pain (m.), bread
palais (m.), palace
par, by, through, out of
parc (m.), park
parce que, because
pardon, excuse me
paresseux, lazy
parler, to speak
parmi, among
parti, departed, set out, started
partout, everywhere
passer, to pass, spend (of time)
pauvre, poor
payer, to pay, to pay for

pays (m.), country, district
pendant, during, for (time)
pendant que, while
penser, to think
perdu, lost
père (m.), father
personne (f.), a person
petit, small, little
peu, little, few
place (f.), place, square, seat
plus, more
poisson (m.), fish
pomme (f.), apple
porte (f.), door, gate
porte-monnaie (m.), purse
porter, to carry, to wear
porteur (m.), porter
pour, for, in order to
pourquoi, why
préférer, to prefer, like better
premier, first
près (*de*), near (to)
prêter, to lend
pris, taken
prix (m.), price, prize
profond, deep
propriétaire (m.), landlord, owner
prudent, prudent, careful
punir, to punish

Q

quand, when
qui, who, which
que, whom, which, that, than,
    what
quel, which, what
quelquechose, something
quelquefois, sometimes
quelqu'un, someone
qu'est-ce qui? What?

R

rapide(ment), rapid(ly)
rapide (m.), fast train
reçu, received
regarder, to look at

régner, to reign
reine (f.), queen
remarquer, to notice
rencontrer, to meet
rendre, to render, give back
repas (m.), meal
représentation (f.), performance
rester, to stay, remain
revenu, come back, returned
roi (m.), king
rouge, red
rue (f.), street

S

salle à manger (f.), dining-room
sans, without
semaine (f.), week
si, if, so
siècle (m.), century
s'il vous plaît, (if you) please
situé, situated
sœur (f.), sister
soir (m.), evening
soldat (m.), soldier
soulier (m.), shoe
sous, under
souvent, often
su, known
sur, on
sûr, sure

T

table (f.), table
tableau (m.), picture
tant, so much
tante (f.), aunt
tasse (f.), cup
temps (m.), time, weather
tête (f.), head
thé (m.) tea
théâtre (m.), theatre
tigre (m.), tiger
timbre-poste (m.), stamp
tirer, to draw, drag, pull
tomber, to fall
touriste (m.), tourist

tout, all
train (m.), train
travail (m.), work
travailler, to work
traverser, to cross
très, very
triste(ment), sad(ly)
trouver, to find
tuer, to kill

U

un(e), a(an), one
usine (f.), factory
utile, useful

V

vacances (f. pl.), holidays
vache (f.), cow
valise (f.), suitcase, bag
vendre, to sell
venu, come
verre (m.), glass
vers, towards
vert, green
viande (f.), meat
vie (f.), life, living
vieux, old
vilain, ugly
village (m.), village
ville (f.), town
vin (m.), wine
visiter, to visit
visiteur (m.), visitor
vite, quickly
vitesse (f.), speed
voie (f.), (railway) track, line
voix (f.), voice
voisin(e),'neighbour, neighbouring
voiture (f.), (motor) car, (railway)
   coach
voler, to steal, to fly
voleur (m.), thief, robber
voyage (m.), journey
voyager, to travel
voyageur (m.), traveller
vrai, true
vu, seen